The Emergence of
Romanticism

The Emergence of
Romanticism

NICHOLAS V. RIASANOVSKY

New York Oxford
OXFORD UNIVERSITY PRESS
1992

Oxford University Press

Oxford   New York   Toronto
Delhi   Bombay   Calcutta   Madras   Karachi
Kuala Lumpur   Singapore   Hong Kong   Tokyo
Nairobi   Dar es Salaam   Cape Town
Melbourne   Auckland   Madrid

and associated companies in
Berlin   Ibadan

Copyright © 1992 by Oxford University Press, Inc.

Published by Oxford University Press, Inc.,
200 Madison Avenue, New York, New York 10016

Library of Congress Cataloging-in-Publication Data
Riasanovsky, Nicholas Valentine, 1923–
The emergence of romanticism / Nicholas V. Riasanovsky.
p. cm.   Includes bibliographical references (p.   ) and index.
ISBN 0-19-507341-X
1. English literature—18th century—History and criticism.
2. Romanticism—Great Britain—History—18th century.
3. German literature—18th century—History and criticism.
4. Literature, Comparative—English and German.
5. Literature, Comparative—German and English.
6. Romanticism—Germany—History—18th century.
7. Christianity and literature.   8. God in literature.   I. Title.
PR447.R48   1992
820.9'145—dc20   91-46113

Permission to reproduce translations of poems from the following works
is gratefully acknowledged:

From *Hymns to the Night* by Novalis, translated by Richard C. Higgins.
Copyright © 1978, 1984, 1988 by Richard C. Higgins, by permission of
the publishers, McPherson & Company, Kingston, New York.

From *Russian Metaphysical Romanticism* by Sarah Pratt. Copyright © 1984
by Stanford University Press. Reprinted by permission.

From *Friedrich Schlegel's Lucinde and the Fragments,* translated by Peter
Firchow. Copyright © 1971 by the University of Minnesota Press.
Reprinted by permission.

1 3 5 7 9 8 6 4 2

Printed in the United States of America
on acid-free paper

To Sir Isaiah Berlin
and the late Dr. H. G. Schenk

Acknowledgments

As I grow older, appropriate acknowledgments become more numerous and crowding. This is especially true of the present study, based as it is on an interest of very long standing and wide compass. Whereas some of my debts can be found in the footnotes—and two even appear in the dedication—others (notably to my wife and to some of my teachers, colleagues, and students) defy precise listing. This paragraph provides merely a skeletal outline, to which must be added my appreciation and gratitude, different in each case but invariably real and memorable. And, as a good custom demands, I want to emphasize that the weaknesses and deficiencies of this work are entirely my own.

Two of my sabbatical years (1984–85 and 1989–90) were devoted primarily to the research and writing of this book. The first I spent as a fellow of the Institute for Advanced Studies in the Behavioral Sciences, located in Stanford, the second at the Smithsonian Institution in Washington, D.C. (with a visit to England) as a Wilson Fellow and a member of the Kennan Institute. I want to acknowledge the fellowships that supported my research during those years, as well as the sabbatical policy of the University of California and the financial and other advantages connected with my chair. This study began as a lecture (later lectures), and I was fortunate to have opportunities to lecture on romanticism at the University of California, Berkeley, and also at Indiana University, the University of Michigan, and the Smithsonian. Libraries were, of course, indispensable for my study, and I profited from the resources of a good number of them, especially the main library at the University of California, Berkeley, and the Library of Congress. At my request, twenty individuals carefully read the manuscript before it was submitted for publication and provided useful corrections and valuable criticisms. They included my wife Arlene and our daughter Maria; five successive research assistants (who performed efficiently a variety of services in furthering my work), namely, Theodore R. Weeks, Joseph B. Mellott, Paul

Holchak, John W. Randolph, Jr., and Ilya Vinkovetsky; doctoral candidate Catherine Evtuhov; Berkeley colleagues Jan de Vries, Martin Jay, Martin Malia, Henry May, Hugh McLean, Robert Middlekauff, Ernest Tuveson, Frederick Wakeman, Jr., and Reginald Zelnik; also professors Herbert Lindenberger of Stanford University, Anthony La Vopa of North Carolina State University, and Sir Isaiah Berlin of Oxford. The index was prepared by Nadine Ghammache and Ilya Vinkovetsky.

Berkeley   N.V.R.
January 1992

Contents

The Emergence of
Romanticism

You cannot see my face, for man shall not see my face and live.

EXOD. 33:20

Introduction

I have been interested in romanticism since childhood. Romanticism meant romantic literature, especially poetry, which I could read in three languages (French, Russian, and English) then and a few others later on. As to romantic thought, ideology, or outlook—call it what you will—although I have always considered it inseparable from poetry, I was eager to learn more about it from whatever source and thus became an avid reader of all kinds of romantic literature as well as literature about romanticism. My Oxford doctoral dissertation, which became my first book, was entitled *Russia and the West in the Teaching of the Slavophiles: A Study of Romantic Ideology.*[1] It presented my view and analysis of that remarkable teaching. Appropriately, I stressed its romantic nature rather than, as in some studies, its links with the spirituality of the Orthodox church or its mirroring of the historical circumstances of a certain kind of Russian educated public of the 1840s.

Slavophilism has remained a lifelong interest; but the attraction of romanticism, more broadly speaking, has also continued. I remember the sudden realization (one day, late in the afternoon, while working on an entirely different subject at the Bibliothèque Nationale) that the obsessive romantic paradox of the finite and the infinite, of one's eternal striving and yet one's inability to reach one's goal did, after all, make sense: it represented the fundamental attitude within the Judeo–Christian tradition of the human being's relationship to God. This would also explain its compulsive power, as well as the fantastic despair of so many great poets and writers, who believed that words failed them and they could not express themselves.

In time, my interest in romanticism became linked to my concern with emergence. Like other intellectual historians, I used freely the concept and framework of *intellectual periods*. For example, my book on the image of Peter the Great[2] was neatly divided: "The Image of Peter the Great in the Russian

---

1. Cambridge, Mass., 1952; German edn., Munich, 1954.
2. *The Image of Peter the Great in Russian History and Thought* (New York, 1985).

Enlightenment, 1700–1826," "The Image of Peter the Great in Russia in the Age of Idealistic Philosophy and Romanticism, 1826–1860," "The Image of Peter the Great in Russia in the Age of Realism and Scholarship, 1860–1917," and "The Image of Peter the Great in the Soviet Union, 1917–1984." It was high time to ask how an intellectual period arose.

As was mentioned earlier, the present book had its origin in lectures; and it still retains that form. Ideally there were three lectures, which now comprise three chapters. In the first I remind the reader of the emergence of romanticism in England; of its central poetry; and, in general, of what I consider most significant about the poetic achievement of Wordsworth and Coleridge, who created English romanticism. In the second, I attempt to do the same for Germany, where romanticism emerged at about the same time. My protagonists in this instance are Novalis, Wackenroder, and Friedrich Schlegel. (I had to sacrifice my two favorite romanticisms, the French and the Russian, because they occurred later and were not present at the emergence.) The extensive citation of romantic poetry (and some prose), together with very brief but pointed accounts of their authors in the first two chapters, are meant to recall forcefully the moment of the emergence of romanticism in European intellectual history, as well as to suggest some central problems of interpretation which it presents. The third chapter, then, aims to explain what actually happened in terms of pantheism or panentheism and the inner content and structure of romantic belief. Narrowly centered on that belief, this chapter is not concerned with the cultural and social evolution of the particular European society which made romanticism possible, or even, to any significant extent, with the long intellectual and religious roots of romantic ideology itself. Although early romanticism is my main focus in this study, I do suggest some of the subsequent, often portentous, lines of development romanticism was to take and how the latter relate to the initial stage. Moreover, I make certain general observations, with appropriate examples, on the nature and structure of romantic thought. I offer some justification, both implicit and explicit, of my rather exclusive selection in the first two chapters of literary personalities and topics—which I consider essential rather than merely representative or illustrative. My presentation ends where it began—with a quotation from a poet.

Among the readers engaged by the press, reader B's explication of my study is so lucid and to the point that I am quoting it in this introduction for the benefit of all who might want to become acquainted with my book. It does not often happen that an author considers a critic's understanding of his work equal to the author's own.

> Nicholas Riasanovsky's *The Emergence of Romanticism* is, as the title implies, a study of the emergence of distinctly "romantic" cultural ethos and literary sensibility. It is an essay in intellectual history (or, in current parlance, "cultural history"), though it draws on a large corpus of literary criticism and

devotes due attention to the literary properties of texts. The essay is also a modest but intriguing exercise in comparative history. Pairing two British authors (Wordsworth and Coleridge) with three German authors (Novalis, Friedrich Schlegel, and Wackenroder), it demonstrates that, for all the cultural differences between them, they represent variations on the same "emergence."

In a field notorious for its murky boundaries and slippery definitions, the author's central argument is refreshingly precise. The "original" Romanticism emerged in England and Germany in the mid-to-late 1790s, and within a decade it had spent itself. If we are to understand both the extraordinary creativity of this initial "burst" and its equally remarkable brevity, we have to come to terms with the early Romanticists' embrace of pantheism (or panentheism). It is in this sense—as an episode in the long history of pantheism—that early Romanticism, at its core, reformulated a religious vision. And it is from the implications of a pantheistic vision that Wordsworth, Coleridge, and their German counterparts recoiled in the opening years of the nineteenth century.

Riasanovsky, it should be stressed, is not arguing that pantheism was one of several vital ingredient of Romanticism, as several other scholars have done. His contention—the one on which the essay's claim to originality stands or falls—is that pantheism was the heart of the beast. The focus on pantheism also distinguishes his approach from efforts to define the essence of Romanticism in psychological terms, as the expression of a psychic structure, or an archetypal myth, or an unconscious urge. Eschewing the a-historical reductionism of such approaches, Riasanovsky treats pantheism as a specific set of ideas with a historical lineage within the Christian tradition.

The essay is fairly brief, as it should be. It was conceived as an interpretive essay and not as a thoroughgoing treatment of Romanticism or even of early Romanticism. It is appropriate to the genre, I think, that the author raises several large issues but considers them outside his agenda. He limits his task to identifying *what* emerged and leaves it to others to explain—in cultural terms, and perhaps even in social terms—*why* it emerged where and when it did. Likewise he does not trace the lineages of Romantic pantheism within the larger pantheistic tradition, though on that score the essay raises a number of interesting questions about eighteenth-century anticipations of Romanticism in British and German Protestantism (and is a welcomed complement to M. H. Abrams's *Natural Supernaturalism*).

The author does suggest, however, that his interpretation may help us understand some of the more puzzling features of Romanticism. If the initial "burst" began with a surge of creativity, it ended with a failure of nerve. In the early Romanticists' pantheistic vision—and here I am summarizing a very subtle argument—the ego either became the One (by appropriating the "external" world as an extension of its creative subjectivity) or was absorbed into the One. In either case, the individual consciousness—even as it was enthralled by its capacity to transcend finitude—confronted the prospect of its annihilation. It was because they were recoiling from that prospect, Riasanovsky suggests, that the early Romanticists could not sustain their initial burst of creativity. For the same reason they tended to find refuge in various forms of political conservatism and religious orthodoxy, despite their initial enthusiasm for the French Revolution. As for the bewildering assortment of nineteenth-century "romanticisms" (with the emphasis on the plural), they appeared precisely because the core—the original pantheistic vision—had been lost. In the absence of the core, other "romantic" elements could enter different combinations with each other and with other cultural trends (including "organic" or integral nationalism, as the author demonstrates nicely by way of Russian romanticism).

The central argument about pantheism is an important one, and the suggested implications will give students of Romanticism much to ponder. Rather than pick at the details of texts, the author effectively constructs his interpretation from an analysis of their larger structures and a nuanced reading of their larger meanings.

I

The Emergence of Romanticism in England

> I wandered lonely as a cloud
> That floats on high o'er vales and hills,
> When all at once I saw a crowd,
> A host, of golden daffodils;
> Beside the lake, beneath the trees,
> Fluttering and dancing in the breeze.
>
> . . .
>
> For oft, when on my couch I lie
> In vacant or in pensive mood,
> They flash upon that inward eye
> Which is the bliss of solitude;
> And then my heart with pleasure fills,
> And dances with the daffodils.
>
> WORDSWORTH,
"I Wandered Lonely as a Cloud"

To quote Wordsworth:

> Up! up! my Friend, and quit your books;
> Or surely you'll grow double:
> Up! up! my Friend, and clear your looks;
> Why all this toil and trouble?
>
> The sun, above the mountain's head,
> A freshening lustre mellow

Through all the long green fields has spread,
His first sweet evening yellow.

Books! 'tis a dull and endless strife:
Come, hear the woodland linnet,
How sweet his music! on my life,
There's more of wisdom in it.

And hark! how blithe the throstle sings!
He, too, is no mean preacher:
Come forth into the light of things,
Let Nature be your Teacher.

She has a world of ready wealth,
Our minds and hearts to bless—
Spontaneous wisdom breathed by health,
Truth breathed by cheerfulness.

One impulse from a vernal wood
May teach you more of man,
Of moral evil and of good,
Than all the sages can.

Sweet is the lore which Nature brings;
Our meddling intellect
Mis-shapes the beauteous forms of things:—
We murder to dissect.

Enough of Science and of Art;
Close up those barren leaves;
Come forth, and bring with you a heart
That watches and receives.[1]

The eye—it cannot choose but see;
We cannot bid the ear be still;
Our bodies feel, where'er they be,
Against or with our will.

Nor less I deem that there are Powers
Which of themselves our minds impress;
That we can feed this mind of ours
In a wise passiveness.

Think you, 'mid all this mighty sum
Of things for ever speaking,
That nothing of itself will come,
But we must still be seeking?

1. William Wordsworth, "The Tables Turned: An Evening Scene on the Same Subject," in his *Poems,* vol. 1, ed. John O. Hayden (Harmondsworth, Eng., 1977), pp. 356–57.

—Then ask not wherefore, here, alone,
Conversing as I may,
I sit upon this old grey stone,
And dream my time away.[2]

Love had he found in huts where poor men lie;
His daily teachers had been woods and rills,
The silence that is in the starry sky,
The sleep that is among the lonely hills.[3]

      —The sky is overcast
With a continuous cloud of texture close,
Heavy and wan, all whitened by the Moon,
Which through that veil is indistinctly seen,
A dull, contracted circle, yielding light
So feebly spread, that not a shadow falls,
Chequering the ground—from rock, plant, tree, or tower.
At length a pleasant instantaneous gleam
Startles the pensive traveller while he treads
His lonesome path, with unobserving eye
Bent earthwards; he looks up—the clouds are split
Asunder,—and above his head he sees
The clear Moon, and the glory of the heavens,
There, in a black-blue vault she sails along,
Followed by multitudes of stars, that, small
And sharp, and bright, along the dark abyss
Drive as she drives: how fast they wheel away,
Yet vanish not!—the wind is in the tree,
But they are silent;—still they roll along
Immeasurably distant; and the vault;
Built round by those white clouds, enormous clouds,
Still deepens its unfathomable depth.
At length the Vision closes; and the mind,
Not undisturbed by the delight it feels,
Which slowly settles into peaceful calm,
Is left to muse upon the solemn scene.[4]

2. From "Expostulation and Reply," in his *Poems,* p. 356.
3. From "Song at the Feast of Brougham Castle upon the Restoration of Lord Clifford, the Shepherd, to the Estates and Honours of His Ancestors," in his *Poems,* p. 730.
4. "A Night-Piece," in his *Poems,* p. 262.

                              —Brook and road
Were fellow-travellers in this gloomy Pass,
And with them did we journey several hours
At a slow step. The immeasurable height
Of woods decaying, never to be decayed,
The stationary blasts of waterfalls,
And in the narrow rent, at every turn,
Winds thwarting winds bewildered and forlorn,
The torrents shooting from the clear blue sky,
The rocks that muttered close upon our ears,
Black drizzling crags that spake by the wayside
As if a voice were in them, the sick sight
And giddy prospect of the raving stream,
The unfettered clouds and region of the heavens,
Tumult and peace, the darkness and the light—
Were all like the workings of one mind, the features
Of the same face, blossoms upon one tree,
Characters of the great Apocalypse,
The types and symbols of Eternity,
Of first, and last, and midst, and without end.[5]

                    —When soft!—the dusky trees between,
And down the path through the open green,
Where is no living thing to be seen;
And through yon gateway, where is found,
Beneath the arch with ivy bound,
Free entrance to the church-yard ground—
Comes gliding in with lovely gleam,
Comes gliding in serene and slow,
Soft and silent as a dream,
A solitary Doe!
White she is as lily of June,
And beauteous as the silver moon
When out of sight the clouds are driven
And she is left alone in heaven;
Or like a ship some gentle day
In sunshine sailing far away,
A glittering ship, that hath the plain
Of ocean for her own domain.[6]

                . . . And I have felt
A presence that disturbs me with the joy

---

5. "The Simplon Pass," in his *Poems*, pp. 637–38.

Of elevated thoughts; a sense sublime
Of something far more deeply interfused,
Whose dwelling is the light of setting suns,
And the round ocean and the living air,
And the blue sky, and in the mind of man:
A motion and a spirit, that impels
All thinking things, all objects of all thought,
And rolls through all things.[7]

There are in our existence spots of time,
That with distinct pre-eminence retain
A renovating virtue, whence—depressed
By false opinion and contentious thought,
Or aught of heavier or more deadly weight,
In trivial occupations, and the round
Of ordinary intercourse—our minds
Are nourished and invisibly repaired;
A virtue, by which pleasure is enhanced,
That penetrates, enables us to mount,
When high, more high, and lifts us up when fallen.[8]

And, turning from her grave, I met
Beside the churchyard yew,
A blooming Girl, whose hair was wet
With points of morning dew.

A basket on her head she bare;
Her brow was smooth and white:
To see a child so very fair,
It was a pure delight!

6. From "The White Doe of Rylstone; or, The Fate of the Nortons," in his *Poems*, p. 746.

7. From "Lines Composed a Few Miles Above Tintern Abbey, on Revisiting the Banks of the Wye During a Tour, July 13, 1798," in his *Poems*, p. 360.

8. From *The Prelude*, in *The Poetical Works of Wordsworth*, rev. ed., ed. Paul D. Sheats (Boston, 1982), p. 210. This celebrated passage from *The Prelude* might remind the reader of the rest, much too long to quote even selectively. As to very numerous commentaries, I found especially suggestive Herbert Lindenberger's emphasis on "this habit of interchanging qualities of the animate and inanimate, of the mind and external nature"; on the slipping from the literal to the figurative or the metaphorical, and back to the literal again; on the dominating images of wind and water, whose chief function of is to act as intermediaries between the two worlds: "From beginning to end Wordsworth is constantly at work finding new ways to invoke the inexpressible" (*On Wordsworth's "Prelude"* [Princeton, 1963] pp. 44, 69, 71, 188). Most recent studies include Mary Jacobus' idiosyncratic analysis, both feminist and psychoanalytic, in her *Romanticism, Writing and Sexual Difference: Essays on "The Prelude"* (Oxford, 1989).

No fountain from its rocky cave
E'er tripped with foot so free;
She seemed as happy as a wave
That dances on the sea.[9]

She dwelt among the untrodden ways
    Beside the springs of Dove,
A Maid whom there were none to praise
    And very few to love:

A violet by a mossy stone
    Half hidden from the eye!
—Fair as a star, when only one
    Is shining in the sky.

She lived unknown, a few could know
    When Lucy ceased to be;
But she is in her grave, and, oh,
    The difference to me![10]

---

9. From "The Two April Mornings," in his *Poems*, vol. 1, pp. 382–83. Compare the following from "Louisa, After Accompanying Her on a Mountain Excursion," in his *Poems*, p. 511.

I met Louisa in the shade,
And, having seen that lovely Maid,
Why should I fear to say
That, nymph-like she is fleet and strong,
And down the rocks can leap along
Like violets in May? . . .

. . .

And, when against the wind she strains,
Oh! might I kiss the mountain rains
That sparkle on her cheek.

Take all that's mine "beneath the moon."
If I with her but half a noon
May sit beneath the walls
Of some old cave, or mossy nook,
When up she winds along the brook
To hunt the waterfalls.

10. "She Dwelt Among the Untrodden Ways," in his *Poems*, p. 366. One critic stressed the hallucinatory quality of the poem based on a strange use of language, i.e., "untrodden ways"; very few to love but none to praise; and "unknown," with but very few to know of her death—no matter or, rather, all the better—"The violet symbolized Lucy and so did the star—and with the two images now forming the terminal extremes of this tremendous new image Lucy inevitably comes to occupy the whole interval between them. Lucy *is* the whole evening scene. . . . What 'She dwelt among the untrodden ways' seems to be *saying*, as a poem, is that the distinctions of the intellect, the water-tight compartments in which we keep violets and stars, our public lives and our private lives, need to be broken down in the interests of a higher reality. It is only

There was a time when meadow, grove, and stream,
The earth, and every common sight,
    To me did seem
    Apparelled in celestial light,
The glory and the freshness of a dream.
It is not now as it has been of yore;—
    Turn whereso'er I may,
    By night or day
The things which I have seen I now can see no more.

    The Rainbow comes and goes,
    And lovely is the Rose;
    The Moon doth with delight
Look round her when the heavens are bare;
    Waters on a starry night
    Are beautiful and fair;
    The sunshine is a glorious birth;
    But yet I know, where'er I go,
That there hath past away a glory from the earth.

· · ·

Wither is fled the visionary gleam?
Where is it now, the glory and the dream?

Our birth is but a sleep and a forgetting:
The Soul that rises with us, our life's Star,
    Hath had elsewhere its setting,
    And cometh from afar.

· · ·

    Hence in a season of calm weather
    Though inland far we be,
Our Souls have sight of that immortal sea
    Which brought us hither,
    Can in a moment travel thither,
And see the Children sport upon the shore,
And hear the mighty waters rolling evermore.

· · ·

I love the Brooks which down their channels fret,
Even more than when I tripped lightly as they;

---

as a symbol of this higher reality that Lucy achieves poetic coherence." (F. W. Bateson, *Wordsworth: A Re-Interpretation* [New York, 1956], pp. 31–34, emphasis in original. Another critic
observed that in the Lucy poems an epitaph upon Lucy becomes a love poem addressed to nature
(Frances Ferguson, *Wordsworth: Language as Counter-Spirit* [New Haven, 1977], pp. 186–87).

The innocent brightness of a new-born Day
    Is lovely yet;
The Clouds that gather round the setting sun
Do take a sober colouring from an eye
That hath kept watch o'er man's mortality;
Another race hath been, and other palms are won.
Thanks to the human heart by which we live,
Thanks to its tenderness, its joys, and fears,
To me the meanest flower that blows can give
Thoughts that do often lie too deep for tears.[11]

One of the great poets of England and the world, Wordsworth has been especially acclaimed as a poet of nature. To appreciate the point it is necessary to rely on reading and rereading the poems themselves rather than on any theoretical expositions. It should be remembered that according to Wordsworth, "poetry is the first and last of all knowledge—it is as immortal as the heart of man."[12] As to analyses, they quickly come up against what Herbert Lindenberger aptly termed the continuous and manifold effort "to invoke the inexpressible." To be sure, elucidations of Wordsworth's poetry are many, and some of them are at least suggestive if not comprehensive or (still less) definitive. Thus, John F. Danby refers to such fundamental experiences as mysticism and falling in love, then continues: "Only, Wordsworth has the experience not with persons but with things, especially with landscapes wherein river, road, wood, mountain, sky and cloud muster their language for a summary utterance. The chief instance of this in Wordsworth's work is maybe 'The Simplon Pass'."[13] Other critics have dwelt on the absorbing,

11. From "Ode: Intimations of Immortality from Recollections of Early Childhood," in his *Poems,* vol. 1, pp. 523–25, 528–29. For one impressive analysis of the poem see Cleanth Brooks, *The Well Wrought Urn: Studies in the Structure of Poetry* (New York, 1947), pp. 114–38, 255–61. Brooks devotes much attention to another notable study in the field, namely, I. A. Richards, *Coleridge on Imagination* (New York, 1950), first published in London in 1934. Compare another celebrated interpretation taking Wordsworth more at his word, namely, Lionel Trilling, *The Liberal Imagination* (Garden City, N.Y., 1953), pp. 130–58.

12. William Wordsworth, "Preface to *Lyrical Ballads,* with Pastoral and Other Poems ('1802')," in his *Poems,* vol. 1, p. 881.

13. John F. Danby, *The Simple Wordsworth: Studies in the Poems, 1797–1807* (London, 1960), p. 118. Cf., e.g., Richard Haven's commentary on "Nutting": "In 'Nutting', for example, the woods are described as figuratively, a woman, and his action as, figuratively, a rape. But to him the woods were alive and virginal; the action *was* a rape" (*Patterns of Consciousness: An Essay on Coleridge* [Amherst, Mass., 1969], p. 177; italics in original). Approaching the subject from the opposite end, so to speak, Stephen Prichett even claimed (much too simply, in my opinion) that during his creative period "Wordsworth had no great interest in nature for its own sake, but only in its metaphorical role as a way of talking about the complexities of man" (*Wordsworth and Coleridge: "The Lyrical Ballads"* (London, 1975), p. 13.

On Wordsworth and nature, see also Alan Grob, *The Philosophic Mind: A Study of Wordsworth's Poetry and Thought, 1797–1805* (Columbus, Ohio, 1973). I disagree with some of the author's main arguments but find passages such as the following highly relevant and incisive: "Internal growth is interpreted essentially as the mind's increasing awareness of tranquility (the human equivalent of the calm of landscape) and as a growing consciousness of the depth and

maternal quality of nature in Wordsworth or on the striking nuptial language in regard to nature which breaks into his poems. Those more intellectually inclined wrote of the metaphysical depth and the philosophical richness of his treatment of nature. All biographies have featured, on excellent evidence, the importance of the outdoors in the poet's life, from early childhood to the time of his death. Wordsworth frequently composed his poems in the open, even in inclement weather; and a certain peregrination formed a leitmotif of his existence. Indeed, in the opinion of one specialist, he even conceived of love in terms of country walks.[14]

There is every reason to believe that nature constituted a constant and major presence in Wordsworth's life. Yet there were also moments (at least during the poet's childhood, adolescence, and creative period) which he immortalized as *spots of time,* when this presence became overwhelming: Wordsworth merged with his vision and entered eternity. Critics have counted more than twenty spots of time in *The Prelude,*[15] and they have been awed by their impact: "*The Prelude* does not merely look forward to authors like Proust, it can hold its own with any of them in the sharpness, vividness, and freshness of its recall of the past. No writing known to me has more compelling power than Wordsworth's accounts of what he happily calls "spots of time": recollected scenes of terror or intense uneasiness from this childhood which seemed to him in his later years paradoxically refreshing."[16] As one commentator tried to elucidate one such Wordsworthian spot of time:

> The psychological process described to De Quincey is evidently, in the light of the comments of the 1815 Preface, the basic material of "There was a Boy." This at any rate is what the poem is supposed to be about. The process, it will be noted, falls into three phases. The first phase is one of

---

extensiveness of one's relational ties with man and nature (the human equivalent of the harmony of landscape). Both of these characteristics have their counterparts, of course, in the poem's symbolically expressed metaphysics, indicating that in *Tintern Abbey,* at least, Wordsworth conceives of the mind's growth as primarily a matter of its correspondence to, or perhaps identity with, nature and hence with the metaphysically real" (pp. 20–21). Cf. John Crowe Ransom, "William Wordsworth: Notes Toward an Understanding of Poetry," in *Wordsworth Centenary Studies Presented at Cornell and Princeton Universities,* ed. Gilbert T. Dunklin (Princeton, 1951), esp. pp. 102–13.

Geoffrey H. Hartman, commenting also on "Tintern Abbey" and suggesting the limits of analysis, writes, "Wordsworth knows one thing only: the affection he bears to nature for its own sake, the quietness and beauty which the presence of nature gives to his mind; and this dialectic of love makes up his entire understanding. The poet thus bears an affection to external nature which cannot be more than stated, nor can the objects of it be more than described" (*The Unmediated Vision: An Interpretation of Wordsworth, Hopkins, Rilke, and Valéry* [New York, 1966], p. 4.

14. Bateson, *Wordsworth,* p. 53.

15. See, e.g., John T. Ogden, "The Structure of Imaginative Experience in Wordsworth's *Prelude,*" *Wordsworth Circle* 6, no. 4 (Autumn 1975): 290–98, esp. 293.

16. Frederick A. Pottle, "Wordsworth in the Present Day," *Proceedings of the American Philosophical Society* 116, no. 6 (December 21, 1972): 447. His is also my favorite commentary on "I Wandered Lonely as a Cloud," namely, "The Eye and the Object in the Poetry of Wordsworth," in *Wordsworth Centenary Studies,* ed. Dunklin (Princeton, 1951).

intense anticipatory concentration on an expected sound or sight. Can he hear the carrier? Will the owls answer? The second phase introduces a relaxation of the attention. The carrier can't be heard. The owls won't answer. The third phase, following immediately on the second, involves the sudden impingement on the consciousness of a different and unexpected sense-impression. Instead of hearing the carrier, Wordsworth sees the star. Instead of hearing the owls, the Boy hears the waterfalls and sees the rocks and the woods and the reflection of the sky in the lake. To this third phase Wordsworth obviously attributed a special significance.[17]

C. M. Bowra, using the concept of the romantic imagination as his main explicatory device, wrote as follows about that last phase:

First, there is Wordsworth's conviction that at times he was in another world which was more real than that of the senses, a world not of sight but of vision. Secondly, his entries into this world were closely connected with his creative and imaginative faculties. It was the justification of his poetry, and he believed that his acquaintance with it was due to his imagination, which, in creating, had moments of visionary clairvoyance. Thirdly, when he had this experience, he felt that he had passed outside time into eternity. He was then so unaware of the common ties of life that he had a timeless exaltation. The three notions are closely allied, though they are distinct enough on analysis. Wordsworth saw them as a single experience and felt a need to explain them.[18]

John T. Ogden made perhaps the most comprehensive attempt to elucidate the "inexpressible" in reference to *The Prelude:*

Between the single event and the development of a lifetime the structure of imaginative experience may be seen unfolding in various intermediate spans of experience. Wordsworth's first summer vacation from Cambridge (Book IV), for example, begins with a lively attentiveness and somewhat fanciful mood, enters into a period of discouragement over "that heartless chase of trivial pleasures," but then concludes with two influential and profound spots of time—the one when the glory of nature left him with unknown vows, the other when an old, discharged soldier provided his view of nature with an appropriate human center. Broader spans of development are evident in the way that Cambridge, London, and France present Wordsworth with obstacles to imagination that ultimately serve to stimulate its activity. His experience with each of these places begins in a mood that is attentive though light-hearted, even fanciful, but it soon shifts into the second stage, which predominates. In each case imagination sleeps (III, 260, 332–34; VII, 468–69; XII, 147). His mood soon becomes troubled by the emptiness, vanity, and perversion that he encounters. His language becomes consciously artificial and satirical to accord with the situation, and his bitterness and frustration increase until, in the case of France, he falls into despair. Each of these

17. Bateson, *Wordsworth,* p. 25.
18. C. M. Bowra, *The Romantic Imagination* (New York, 1961), p. 94.

experiences, however, prepares Wordsworth for a succeeding stage of illumination and fulfillment: Cambridge is followed by summer vacation, where he gains a human-heartedness to his love (IV, 233). After his stay in London he attains a new perspective that elevated his view of human nature (VIII, 644–75). The disaster of the French Revolution forces him into the realization that political reform depends upon moral reform, which in turn depends upon a reform of sensibility, which he as a poet can hope to effect.

Regardless of the span of time involved—whether a moment, several months, several years, or thirty-five years—the structure of imaginative experience involves the same sequence of four stages.

The process of recollection (as it may be distinguished from the faculty of memory) is also based on the same structure.

Poetic composition, which Wordsworth allies with reflection, is itself based on the structure of imaginative experience. . . . First, "poetry . . . takes its origin from emotion recollected in tranquility." Secondly, "by a species of reaction, the tranquility gradually disappears." Thirdly, "an emotion kindred to that which was before the subject of contemplation, is gradually produced, and does itself actually exist in the mind." This emotion wells into "the spontaneous overflow of powerful feelings" which, finally, becomes the poem (*P[oetical] W[orks]*, II, 400–401). While composition begins in tranquility, it rises to an excitement that may be as intense as, or even more intense than, the original experience was.

The four-stage structure of imaginative experience thus governs both the momentary experience and the experience of a lifetime; it governs the primary experience as well as the reflected and poetized experience. The four stages of the single "spot of time" are a miniature version of the four ages of man's life. The "spot of time" is the individual cell of experience, and it has the same basic structure as the whole body of experience that makes up the total life of man.

Ogden went on to explain that the four-stage structure of imaginative experience central to Wordsworth's creativity could also be found in the dynamics of religious conversion, secular love, problem solving, and Gestalt perception and that it was this universal law of the human mind which Wordsworth sought to express in his poetry.[19]

Spots of time usually began in surprise and fear and ended in transcendent bliss. And they seemed to be intrinsically connected with Wordsworth's peculiar ability to transmute human passions and human suffering into a supreme contemplative tranquility. In the words of a perceptive student of this

19. Quoted and summarized from Ogden, "Structure," pp. 295–97. The *Poetical Works* cited is the edition of E. de Selincourt and Helen Darbishire, 5 vols. (Oxford, 1940–49). Many critics shared Ogden's view of the central significance of the spots of time, although they eschewed attempts to explain them. For example, B. Ifor Evans wrote: "There remains one matter compared with which all else is of minor importance. It is that Wordsworth did at times reach an order of mystical vision in poetry which is of a quality without parallel in our literature, which cannot be explained in reference to psychology or philosophy, and which makes all his views on politics comparatively unimportant." ("Wordsworth and the European Problem of the Twentieth Century," in *Wordsworth Centenary Studies,* ed. Dunklin, p. 127).

subject, James H. Averill: "The poetry of 'human passions, human characters, and human incidents' is for Wordsworth inevitably the poetry of suffering. He does not avert his eyes from wretchedness; quite the contrary, he
seems fascinated by it. The *Lyrical Ballads* and the narrative poems from
'Salisbury Plane' to 'The White Doe of Rylstone' brood upon 'Sorrow that is
not sorrow, but delight / And miserable love that is not pain / To hear of'."[20]
Indeed, "in Wordsworth's poetry, guilt, fear, grief, remembered terror, or
intense response to nature,—virtually any powerful emotion it would seem—
is able to move the mind to profound tranquility."[21] Averill convincingly
emphasizes the links between Wordsworth and sentimentalism and affirms
that "Wordsworth draws more from the sentimental movement than does
any other major English Romantic poet."[22] Yet I doubt his assertion that the
relevant Wordsworthian texts are different from those of the sentimentalists
only "in degree rather than in kind."[23] What is new is precisely the strange
central dynamic of Wordsworth's creativity. Numerous other critics have
noted the fundamental calming effect which nature exercised on Wordsworth;
and some drew parallels between the emotional sequence in many of the
poems and the poet's own escape into nature from his disastrous experiences
with Annette Vallon and the French Revolution. Still, it would be at least
equally legitimate to consider these last two phenomena as merely temporary
intruders into a more basic Wordsworthian creative rhythm.

Whatever the exact beginnings of the spots of time, they ended in bliss;
and this bliss may well be regarded as the central experience of Wordsworth's
creativity and life.[24] Its transcendent importance contributed to the monu-
mental seriousness of the poet's work. Even in daily existence Wordsworth
"was never popular, but by those who knew him he was revered, and felt to
be a person somewhat apart, endowed with unusual powers and possessing a

20. James H. Averill, *Wordsworth and the Poetry of Human Suffering,* (Ithaca, N.Y., 1980), p. 10.
See also Cleanth Brooks, "Wordsworth and Human Suffering: Notes on Two Early Poems," in
From Sensibility to Romanticism, ed. Frederick W. Hillers and Harold Bloom (New York, 1965),
pp. 373–87.

21. Averill, *Wordsworth and the Poetry,* p. 90.

22. Ibid., p. 10. For a particularly brilliant presentation of one link among Wordsworth,
Coleridge, and earlier English literature, see M. H. Abrams, "Structure and Style in the Greater
Romantic Lyric," in *From Sensibility,* ed. Hillers and Bloom, pp. 527–60.

23. Averill, *Wordsworth and the Poetry,* p. 54.

24. The creative process itself—composing poetry—was a painful and exhausting task for
Wordsworth, as is richly attested by himself, his sister and closest associate Dorothy, and others:
"Poetic excitement, when accompanied by protracted labour in composition has through-out
my life brought on more or less bodily derangement" (Wordsworth, *Poetical Works,* ed. Selincourt and Darbishire, vol. 3, p. 542). George McLean Harper even wrote in his well-known
biography that "William composed under demonic influence, and at such times Dorothy with-
drew to suffer in silent fear" (*William Wordsworth: His Life, Works, and Influence,* 2 vols. [1929;
reprint, New York, 1960], vol. 2, p. 363. See also the latest major biography, Stephen Gill,
William Wordsworth: A Life (Oxford, 1989) and Mary Moorman's rich and sensitive *William
Wordsworth: A Biography* (Oxford, 1957, 1965). For a detailed chronology consult Mark L. Reed,
Wordsworth: The Chronology of the Early Years, 1770–1799 (Cambridge, Mass., 1967);
idem, *Wordsworth: A Chronology of the Middle Years, 1800–1815* (Cambridge, Mass., 1975).

certain moral grandeur."[25] Ineffable on its fundamental level, the experience led on other levels to supreme, all-encompassing artistic and philosophical projects, which never advanced beyond mere plans or, at best (and that best could be very good indeed), "preludes."[26]

Moreover, the vision tended to embrace and monopolize all of Wordsworth. Little was left for other human beings: "There is an almost Miltonic aloofness about Wordsworth. His constant theme may be the mind of men, but it is conceived in terms of such grandeur that it becomes inhuman. He may be preoccupied with the emotions of the individual, but the very fact that they are *so* important to him lifts them from the level of personal experience. He may be the poet of the ordinary and everyday, but the claims he makes for it are too odd to be sympathetic."[27] Shelley referred to Wordsworth as "a solemn and unsexual man."[28] A contemporary reviewer lamented: "Gretchen, Rica, Lilli—what reader of the *Dichtung und Wahrheit* can ever forget these dead German maidens, or their influence on the life of Goethe? But not one such love-experience of our English author is there recorded in *The Prelude.*"[29]

Another critic of *The Prelude* reinforced the point: "In Shelley again—we are contrasting not his poetry but his idiosyncrasy with that of Wordsworth—we encounter in its full vigour the erotic element of poetry, the absence of which in Wordsworth is so remarkable, that of all poets of equal rank and power in other respects, he, and he alone, may be said to have dispensed with it altogether. The sensuous element was omitted in his composition."[30] A third wrote still more generally and more tellingly:

> The chapters of the poem might have been very properly entitled, "Moods in Boyhood," "Moods in Cambridge," "Moods among my Books," "Moods among the Alps," "Moods in France," etc. Characters, indeed, rush occasionally across those moods. Now it is his humble "dame"—now it is his amiable sister—now it is a friend of youth, departed—and now the "rapt one with the Godlike forehead," the wondrous Coleridge, but they come like shadows, and like shadows depart, nor does their presence prevail f · more than a moment to burst the web of the great soliloquy. Indeed, whether with them or without them, among mountains or men, with his faithful terrier, and talking to himself by the wayside, or pacing the Palais Royal, Wordsworth is equally and always alone.[31]

25. Moorman, *Wordsworth*, vol. 1, p. 266.

26. Thus, Bateson cites *The Recluse* as the projected philosophic magnum opus which haunted Wordsworth till his death (*Wordsworth*, p. 138).

27. Jonathan Wordsworth, *The Music of Humanity: A Critical Study of Wordsworth's "Ruined Cottage" Incorporating Texts from a Manuscript of 1799–1800* (London, 1969), p. 50; italics in original.

28. Quoted in Pottle, *Wordsworth*, p. 443.

29. William Wordsworth, *"The Prelude," 1799, 1805, 1850*, ed. Jonathan Wordsworth, M. H. Abrams, and Stephen Gill (New York, 1979), p. 556.

30. Ibid., p. 552.

31. Ibid., pp. 549–50.

Or, in the words of a modern specialist commenting on the poet's stay in Germany, "It is characteristic of Wordsworth's complete isolation from human society at this time that the one inhabitant of Germany for whom he felt any affection was a bird."[32] George McLean Harper repeatedly regrets this characteristic in his two-volume biography: "Indeed, the enjoyment of natural beauty was apparently his one absorbing passion."[33] Coleridge, a rapt admirer of Wordsworth, nevertheless referred to his "dramatic ventriloquism," that is, his consistent inability to dramatize anyone but himself.[34] The most famous capsule summary of Wordsworth's remarkable stance in literature and life is Keats's "egotistical sublime." In any case, one should look beyond mere insensitivity or arrogance: "Wordsworth's egotism cannot be called misanthropy, it is nearer to solipsism."[35]

Yet isolation did not necessarily mean weakness. (The egotistical was, after all, sublime.) Not inappropriately, Dorothy named a rocky peak after her brother.[36] Moorman's reference to "a certain moral grandeur" finds ample support in memoirs and letters of contemporaries. They were especially impressed by Wordsworth's "constant and firm persuasion of his own *greatness.*"[37] The "dedicated spirit" of *The Prelude* never doubted the immensity of his calling or his role. To those around him this natural conviction could be

32. Bateson, *Wordsworth,* p. 149. The bird was a kingfisher. Compare Wordsworth's poem of 1846, "I Know an Aged Man Constrained to Dwell," where the protagonist, apparently impervious to human contact, has his only emotional attachment to a redbreast. (*Poems,* vol. 2, p. 898).

33. Harper, *William Wordsworth,* vol. 1, p. 57. Harper's narrative is sprinkled with such passages as the following: "By curiosities he means natural objects of interest. As at Orleans what he thought most worthy of record was a babbling spring, so here [Sockburn, Cumberland, and Westmorland], he cared more for waterfalls, gorges, peaks, and dales, than for the works of man" (vol. 2, pp. 301–2).

34. Quoted in Oscar James Campbell and Paul Mueschke, " 'Guilt and Sorrow': A Study in the Genesis of Wordsworth's Aesthetic," *Modern Philology* 23 (Feb. 1926): 304.

35. Bateson, *Wordsworth,* p. 202. One is reminded of Irving Babbitt's dictum, "There is in fact no object in the romantic universe—only subject" (*Rousseau and Romanticism* [Boston, 1919], p. 225). This image of Wordsworth is widespread and, in my opinion, strongly supported by evidence; but it certainly has not remained unchallenged. For one especially interesting effort to "humanize" Wordsworth (especially interesting because immediately linked to primary sources), see William and Mary Wordsworth, *The Love Letters of William and Mary Wordsworth,* ed. Beth Darlington (Ithaca, N.Y., 1981). For the opposite view, see David Ferry, *The Limits of Mortality: An Essay on Wordsworth's Major Poems* (Middletown, Conn., 1959). Ferry concluded: "His genius was his enmity to man, which he mistook for love, and his mistake led him into confusions which he could not bear. But when he banished the confusions, he banished his distinctive greatness as well" (p. 173).

36. On that occasion and the relevant poem, see Moorman, *William Wordsworth,* p. 464. Compare Wordsworth's own statement, "I would *allegorize* myself, as a Rock with it's [*sic*] summit just raised above the surface of some Bay or Strait in the Arctic Sea" (quoted in Geoffrey H. Hartman, "Reflections on the Evening Star: Akenside to Coleridge," in *New Perspectives on Coleridge and Wordsworth,* ed. Geoffrey H. Hartman [New York, 1972], p. 119; italics in original).

37. Wordsworth, *"Prelude" 1799, 1805, 1850,* p. 538; italics in original. According to a hostile critic in the *Satirist,* "Fond as he is of the words *nature, modesty, simplicity,* etc., this author perpetually betrays the most magnificent opinions of his own powers" (quoted in John E. Jordan, *Why the "Lyrical Ballads"? The Background, Writing, and Character of Wordsworth's 1798 "Lyrical Ballads"* [Berkeley, 1976], p. 100; italics in original).

amazing, awkward, unsettling, even ridiculous, but as Coleridge and others attested, it could be as well compelling, overwhelming, almost divine.

II

Then there was Coleridge. "*Samuel Taylor Coleridge,* born in Devon in 1772 and educated at Christ's Hospital and Jesus College, Cambridge. Settled near Wordsworth at Nether Stowey in Somerset in 1797, issued *Lyrical Ballads* with him in 1798, travelled in Germany (1798–9), settled at Keswick in 1800, and finally at Highgate in 1816. Died in 1834."[38] Also one of the great poets of England and the world.

> And what if all of animated nature
> Be but organic Harps diversely fram'd
> That tremble into thought, as o'er them sweeps
> Plastic and vast, one intellectual breeze,
> At once the Soul of each, and God of all?[39]

> Ah! slowly sink
> Behind the western ridge, thou glorious Sun!
> Shine in the slant beams of the sinking orb,
> Ye purple heath-flowers! richlier burn, ye clouds!
> Live in the yellow light, ye distant groves!
> And kindle, thou blue Ocean! So my friend
> Struck with deep joy may stand, as I have stood,
> Silent with swimming sense; yea, gazing round
> On the wide landscape, gaze till all doth seem
> Less gross than bodily; and of such hues
> As veil the Almighty Spirit, when yet he makes
> Spirits perceive his presence.[40]

> "Most musical, most melancholy" bird!
> A melancholy bird? Oh! idle thought!
> In Nature there is nothing melancholy.
> But some night-wandering man whose heart was pierced

38. Samuel Taylor Coleridge, *Biographia Literaria; or, Biographical Sketches of My Literary Life and Opinions,* ed. George Watson (London, 1960), unn. p; italics in original. The most recent biographies of Coleridge are Stephen M. Weissman, M.D., *His Brother's Keeper: A Psychobiography of Samuel Taylor Coleridge* (Madison, Conn., 1988) and Richard Holmes, *Coleridge: Early Visions* (London, 1989), which is to be completed by a second volume. See also Richard Holmes's shorter study, *Coleridge* (Oxford, 1982).

39. From "The Eolian Harp" in *Coleridge: Poetical Works,* ed. Ernest Hartley Coleridge (Oxford, 1969), p. 102.

40. From "This Lime-Tree Bower My Prison" in *Coleridge: Poetical Works,* pp. 179–80.

With the remembrance of a grievous wrong,
Or slow distemper, or neglected love,
(And so, poor wretch! filled all things with himself,
And made all gentle sounds tell back the tale
Of his own sorrow) he, and such as he,
First named these notes a melancholy strain.[41]

Hast thou a charm to stay the morning-star
In his steep course? So long he seems to pause
On thy bald awful head, O sovran *Blanc,*
The Arve and Arveiron at thy base
Rave ceaselessly; but thou, most awful Form!
Risest from forth thy silent sea of pines,
How silently,! Around thee and above
Deep is the air and dark, substantial, black,
And ebon mass: methinks thou piercest it,
As with a wedge! But when I look again,
It is thine own calm home, thy crystal shrine,
Thy habitation from eternity!
O dread and silent Mount! I gazed upon thee,
Till thou, still present to the bodily sense,
Didst vanish from my thought: entranced in prayer
I worshipped the Invisible alone.

    Yet, like some sweet beguiling melody,
So sweet, we know not we are listening to it,
Thou, the meanwhile wast blending with my Thought,
Yea, with my life and Life's own secret joy:
Till the dilating Soul, enrapt, transfused,
Into the mighty vision passing—there
As in her natural form, swelled vast to Heaven!

. . .

    Ye ice-falls! ye that from the mountain's brow
Adown enormous ravines slope amain—
Torrents, methinks, that heard a mighty voice,
And stopped at once amid their maddest plunge!
Motionless torrents! silent cataracts!
Who made you glorious as the Gates of Heaven
Beneath the keen full moon? Who bade the sun
Clothe you with rainbows? Who, with living flowers
Of loveliest blue, spread garlands at your feet?—
God! let the torrents, like a shout of nations,
Answer! and let the ice-plains echo, God!

41. From "The Nightingale" in *Coleridge: Poetical Works,* p. 264.

God! sing ye meadow-streams with gladsome voice!
Ye pine-groves, with your soft and soul-like sounds!
And they too have a voice, yon piles of snow,
And in their perilous fall shall thunder, God!

. . .

   Thou too, hoar Mount! with thy sky-painting peaks,
Oft from whose feet the avalanche, unheard,
Shoots downward, glittering through the pure serene
Into the depth of clouds, that veil thy breast—
Thou too again, stupendous Mountain! thou
That as I raise my head, awhile bowed low
In adoration, upward from thy base
Slow travelling with dim eyes suffused with tears,
Solemnly seemest, like a vapoury cloud,
To rise before me—Rise, O ever rise,
Rise like a cloud of incense from the Earth!
Thou kingly Spirit throned among the hills,
Thou dread ambassador from Earth to Heaven,
Great Hierarch! tell thou the silent sky,
And tell the stars, and tell yon rising sun
Earth, with her thousand voices, praises God. [42]

Beyond the shadow of the ship,
I watched the water-snakes:
They moved in tracks of shining white,
And when they reared, the elfish light
Fell off in hoary flakes.

Within the shadow of the ship,
I watched their rich attire:
Blue, glossy green, and velvet black,
They coiled and swam: and every track
Was a flash of golden fire.

O happy living things! no tongue
Their beauty might declare:
A spring of love gushed from my heart,
And I blessed them unaware.

The self-same moment I could pray;
And from my neck so free
The Albatross fell off, and sank
Like lead into the sea.

---

  42. From "Hymn Before Sun-Rise in the Vale of Chamouni" in *Coleridge: Poetical Works,*
pp. 376–80; emphasis in original.

PART V.

Oh Sleep! it is a gentle thing,
Beloved from pole to pole!
To Mary Queen the praise be given!
She sent the gentle sleep from Heaven,
That slid into my soul.

The silly buckets on the deck,
That had so long remained,
I dreamt that they were filled with dew;
And when I awoke, it rained.

My lips were wet, my throat was cold,
My garments all were dank;
Sure I had drunken in my dreams,
And still my body drank.

I moved and could not feel my limbs:
I was so light—almost
I thought that I had died in sleep,
And was a blessèd ghost.

. . .

Around, around, flew each sweet sound
Then darted to the Sun;
Slowly the sounds came back again,
Now mixed, now one by one.

Sometimes a-dropping from the sky
I heard the sky-lark sing;
Sometimes all little birds that are,
How they seemed to fill the sea and air
With their sweet jargoning!

And now 'twas like all instruments,
Now like a lonely flute;
And now it is an angel's song,
That makes the heavens be mute.

It ceased; yet still the sails made on
A pleasant noise till noon,
A noise like of a hidden brook
In the leafy month of June,
That to the sleeping woods all night
Singeth a quiet tune.

. . .

Farewell, farewell! but this I tell
To thee, thou Wedding Guest!

He prayeth well, who loveth well
Both man and bird and beast.

He prayeth best, who loveth best
All things both great and small;
For the dear God who loveth us,
He made and loveth all.[43]

A damsel with a dulcimer
In a vision once I saw:
It was an Abyssinian maid,
And on her dulcimer she played,
Singing of Mount Abora.
Could I revive within me
Her symphony and song,
To such a deep delight 'twould win me,
That with music loud and long
I would build that dome in air,
That sunny dome! those caves of ice!
And all who heard should see them there,
And all should cry, Beware! Beware!
His flashing eyes, his floating hair!
Weave a circle round him thrice,
And close your eyes with holy dread,
For he on honey-dew hath fed,
And drunk the milk of Paradise.[44]

There was a time when earth, and sea, and skies,
    The bright green vale, and forest's dark recess,
With all things, lay before mine eyes
    In steady loveliness:
But now I feel, on earth's uneasy scene,
    Such sorrows as will never cease;—
    I only ask for peace;
If I must live to know that such a time has been!![45]

A grief without a pang, void, dark, and drear,
    A stifled, drowsy, unimpassioned grief,
    Which finds no natural outlet, no relief,
        In word, or sigh, or tear—

---

43. From "The Rime of the Ancient Mariner" in *Coleridge: Poetical Works,* pp. 198–201, 209.
44. From "Kubla Khan" in *Coleridge: Poetical Works,* p. 298.
45. From "The Mad Monk" in *Coleridge: Poetical Works,* p. 348.

> O Lady! in this wan and heartless mood,
> To other thoughts by yonder throstle woo'd
>   All this long eve, so balmy and serene,
> Have I been gazing on the western sky,
>   And its peculiar tint of yellow green:
> And still I gaze—and with how blank an eye'.
> And those thin clouds above, in flakes and bars,
> That give away their emotion to the stars;
> Now sparkling, now bedimmed, but always seen:
> Yon crescent Moon, as fixed as if it grew
> In its own cloudless, starless lake of blue;
> I see them all so excellently fair,
> I see, not feel, how beautiful they are!
>
> O Lady! we receive but what we give,
> And in our life alone does Nature live.[46]

Coleridge's poetry of nature, spirit, and related subjects was as memorable and distinctive as Wordsworth's, though more problematic and at times very difficult to understand and interpret. Of course, there were major similarities between what the two poets produced, which made their most remarkable cooperation possible. A reading of, for example, "Hymn Before Sun-rise in the Vale of Chamouni" and "The Simplon Pass" immediately suggests the great extent to which the two pieces belong to the same universe. Again, if Lindenberger and other critics are correct in emphasizing wind and water as the central presences in Wordsworth's poetry, and as mediators between the two worlds in constant interchange, they also stream triumphantly through Coleridge's poems, "The Rime of the Ancient Mariner" may be cited as possibly the most singular and noteworthy example in literature of the interaction of the two worlds. M. H. Abrams referred to Coleridge's "crowning metaphor of an eddy. The figure implies a ceaseless and circular interchange of life between soul and nature in which it is impossible to distinguish what is given from what is received: 'To her may all things live, from pole to pole / Their life the eddying of her living soul!' "[47] Coleridge often reacted to the nature around him apparently very much like Wordsworth. In particular, he wrote to his brother on March 10, 1798: "I love fields and woods and mounta[ins] with almost a visionary fondness—and because I have found benevolence and quietness growing within me as that fondness [has] increased, therefore I should wish to be the means of implanting it in others."[48]

---

46. From "Dejection: An Ode" in *Coleridge: Poetical Works,* pp. 364–65.

47. M. H. Abrams, *The Mirror and the Lamp: Romantic Theory and the Critical Tradition* (New York, 1953), p. 68. The lines of poetry are from "Dejection."

48. Quoted in William Wordsworth and Samuel Taylor Coleridge, *Lyrical Ballads: Wordsworth and Coleridge.* Raymond L. Brett and Alun R. Jones (London, 1963), p. xxi; material within square brackets supplied by the editors. Compare, for instance, "I do not think it possible, that any bodily pains could eat out the love and joy, that is so substantially part of me, towards hills,

But there were also differences, even at their closest approach, between the visions of the two great poets. Like Wordsworth, Coleridge sought and found culmination in ecstasy: "For Coleridge, as for Collins, ecstasy and the vision of truth are the same, and they constitute the true sublime."[49] Yet somehow, as almost every commentator has noted, the cerebral element is almost always more prominent in Coleridge than in Wordsworth, who remains the quintessential poet of feeling. Perhaps in connection with that, Coleridge has fewer spots of time—and these less effective in absorbing and transmuting the conflicts and the tensions into a supreme unity. Of the poet's most famous three pieces marking the apogee of his genius, "Christabel" is a striking and (to me) highly disturbing study in evil. I do not understand the unforgettable magical message of "Kubla Khan," but a number of commentators have also linked it to evil, at least in important part. "The Rime of the Ancient Mariner" is indeed a story of redemption; but it is a complex, unclear, and perhaps incomplete story.

> "It is he?" quoth one, "Is this the man?
> By him who died on cross,
> With his cruel bow he laid full low
> The harmless Albatross.
>
> The spirit who bideth by himself
> In the land of mist and snow,
> He loved the bird that loved the man
> Who shot him with his bow."
>
> The other was a softer voice,
> As soft as honey-dew:
> Quoth he, "The man hath penance done,
> And penance more will do."[50]

In a sense, Coleridge kept repenting all his life. Unlike Wordsworth, he had none of the imposing self-assurance and grandeur of his friend. On the

---

and rocks, and steep waters!" (quoted in Holmes, *Coleridge: Early Visions,* p. 343). On the creation, setting, and reception of the *Lyrical Ballads* see especially Jordan, *Why the "Lyrical Ballads"?*

49. J. B. Beer, *Coleridge the Visionary* (London, 1959), p. 197. Richard Haven in particular emphasized the experiential nature of Coleridge's art and thought: "The speculation follows from the experience"; "The Mariner's voyage is not speculative theory but psychological fact"; "He is not simply attempting a logical reconciliation of the notions of finite man and infinite God, but is rather attempting to state the relations implied in the *experience* of being, of finiteness and infinity, alienation and union"; etc. (*Patterns,* pp. 78, 109, 131; italics in original). As to literary sources of Coleridge's great visionary poems, the extensive literature includes John Livingston Lowes's enduring classic, *The Road to Xanadu: A Study in the Ways of the Imagination* (Boston, 1927).

50. Coleridge, *Coleridge: Poetical Works,* p. 202. The sense of unease, so pervasive in Coleridge, is interestingly analyzed with regard to space in Michael G. Cooke, "The Manipulation of Space in Coleridge's Poetry," in *New Perspectives,* ed. Hartman.

contrary, he held himself and his work in low esteem.[51] A magnificent conversationalist and a man of great charm, Coleridge was continuously unhappy in his personal life, chronically ill, and for many years lasting until his death a drug addict.[52] As he stated his case in the epitaph which he wrote for himself on November 9, 1833, and which was first published in 1834, the year of his death:

> Stop, Christian passer-by!—Stop, child of God,
> And read with gentle breast. Beneath this sod
> A poet lies, or that which once seem'd he.
> O, lift one thought in prayer for S.T.C.;
> That he who many a year with toil of breath
> Found death in life, may here find life in death!
> Mercy for praise—to be forgiven for fame
> He ask'd, and hoped, through Christ. Do thou the same![53]

And it was Coleridge who felt the weight of Christ's injunction in that "we must not only love our neighbours as ourselves, but ourselves likewise as our neighbors."[54]

---

51. Walter Jackson Bate comparing Coleridge to other major European poets since the Renaissance, in his standard biography (notable for its fine sensitivity to its subject), even argued, "To begin with, no other poet of comparable stature has devoted so little time and effort to his poetry. Second, and more important, none has considered it so incidental to his other interests, hopes, or anxieties" (*Coleridge,* [London, 1968], p. 40). The claim seems plausible, although one may think of other strong contenders, such as the equally great Russian romantic poet Tiutchev.

As to the general comparison of—or, rather, contrast between—Wordsworth and Coleridge as human beings and romantic intellectuals, I am strongly reminded of a similar striking contrast between two Russian romanticists, Aleksei Stepanovich Khomiakov and Ivan Vasilievich Kireevskii, founders of Slavophilism and major figures in the history of thought in Russia, although not writers of the same stature as the two Englishmen. On Khomiakov and Kireevskii, see my *Russia and the West in the Teaching of the Slavophiles: A Study of Romantic Ideology* (Cambridge, Mass., 1952), esp. pp. 34–46. In Coleridge's own words, "If I might so say, I am as an *acting* man, a creature of mere Impact" (quoted in Holmes, *Coleridge: Early Visions,* p. 315; italics in original).

52. The issue of opium addiction has been an important one for students of Coleridge because opium almost certainly affected his creative work, notably his poetry. Its strangeness and magic, as well as such specifics as the colors in "The Rime of the Ancient Mariner" and the landscape in "Kubla Khan," have been ascribed to that drug. As an introduction to the subject, see, e.g., Robert Cecil Bald, "Coleridge and 'The Ancient Mariner': Addenda to *The Road to Xanadu,*" in *Nineteenth-Century Studies,* ed. Herbert Davis, William C. DeVane, and Robert C. Bald (Ithaca, N.Y., 1940). Still, most Coleridge specialists detect an intrinsic internal unity in the poet's life and oeuvre, with or without drugs. Possibly, opium fitted Coleridge more than it shaped him. For the latest expert treatment of the topic, see doctor Weissman, *His Brother's Keeper.*

53. Coleridge, *Coleridge: Poetical Works,* pp. 491–92. The editor noted that in the next to the last line *for* is used twice in the sense of "instead of." Coleridge defined prayer as "the effort to connect the misery of the self with the blessedness of God" (quoted in J. Robert Barth, *Coleridge and Christian Doctrine* [Cambridge, Mass., 1969], p. 182).

54. Coleridge, *Biographia Literaria,* p. 281.

III

The relationship between Wordsworth and Coleridge was of a unique kind and importance in literature. Perhaps the most perceptive student of the subject, Thomas McFarland began his chapter on "The Symbiosis of Coleridge and Wordsworth" as follows:

> The intellectual relationship of Coleridge and Wordsworth has scarcely any cultural counterpart. It is almost impossible to bring to mind any other two figures, so important each in his own right, but also so dependent the one upon the other during his richest intellectual years. The interchange between Goethe and Schiller occurred after each had established his own reputation and his own mode. That between Socrates and Plato was the relationship of master to pupil, while that between Plato and Aristotle, likewise a master–pupil situation, involved fundamental disagreements. The relationship of Beaumont and Fletcher was perhaps as close as that of Coleridge and Wordsworth, but in this instance neither figure achieved major stature in his own right.
>
> But Coleridge and Wordsworth not only profoundly influenced one another; they did so in a way that challenges ordinary methods of assessment.

One critic, McFarland continued, recorded the appearance of so many "Wordsworthian" lines in Coleridge that he began to wonder how much Wordsworth there was in Coleridge. Another emphasized the ensuing inseparability of the critical work of the two writers, noting that *The Prelude* had been a letter to Coleridge and *Biographia Literaria* Coleridge's reply.[55]

The historic cooperation between Coleridge and Wordsworth was based especially on Coleridge's extraordinary receptivity and in certain ways even submissiveness in his relationship with his formidable friend. As Walter Jackson Bate explained, "Throughout most of his life the unconfident Coleridge—inhibited when he tried to write directly and formally in his own voice (inhibited, that is, when he was trying to write anything he felt really important)—became most completely alive and the resources of his mind most open when he could talk or write vicariously."[56] Or, in McFarland's words, "It seems clear, in short, that Coleridge's deep masochism not only asserted itself in repeated vices of procrastination, repeated indulgences in hypochondria, and repeated improprieties of 'plagiarism', but also made him uncannily able to subordinate himself to the style of his friend."[57] Together

---

55. Thomas McFarland, *Romanticism and the Forms of Ruin: Wordsworth, Coleridge, and Modalities of Fragmentation* (Princeton, N.J., 1981), pp. 56–57. McFarlands references are to H. M. Margouliouth, *Wordsworth and Coleridge—1795–1834* (London, 1955), pp. 93–94, and James Heffernan, *Wordsworth's Theory of Poetry: The Transforming Imagination* (Ithaca, N.Y., 1969), p. 5, respectively. For another scholarly and perceptive account of the relationship of the two poets, see Earl Leslie Griggs, "Wordsworth Through Coleridge's Eyes," in *Wordsworth Centenary Studies*, ed. Dunklin.

56. Bate, *Coleridge*, p. 37.

57. McFarland, *Romanticism*, p. 59.

with that went, of course, Coleridge's overwhelming regard for Wordsworth, "the first and greatest philosophical Poet."[58] Even when Coleridge measured his judgment of his associate, the measuring was very impressive: "In imaginative power, he stands nearest of all modern writers to Shakespeare and Milton; and yet in a kind perfectly unborrowed and his own."[59] He dismissed the contemporary criticism and lack of appreciation of his hero with the remark that "his fame belongs to another age, and can neither be accelerated nor retarded."[60]

The ensuing "dialogical interchange between the poetic productions of Wordsworth and Coleridge"[61] is brilliantly depicted by McFarland, although the critic is not necessarily convincing in every particular.[62] In the case of "The Rime of the Ancient Mariner" he stresses (like others before him) Wordsworth's participation in the very emergence and planning of the poem, as well as in its actual composition but concludes that it belonged essentially to Coleridge.[63] McFarland uses another illustration:

> A more complicated kind of interaction existed between Wordsworth's "The Rainbow," his "Intimations Ode," and Coleridge's "Dejection: An Ode" on the one hand, and Coleridge's "Dejection" and Wordsworth's "Resolution and Independence" on the other. Briefly stated, the matter is this: Coleridge's "Dejection" was probably an answer to the philosophy of joy from nature expressed by "The Rainbow" and the "Intimations Ode"; "Resolution and Independence" was probably a correction of the despondency of the first version of "Dejection"; and the revised version of "Dejection" that was published on Wordsworth's wedding day became a kind of wedding gift and affectionate acquiescence in the philosophy of joy once more.

McFarland proceeds to support his argument by a close examination of the chronology of the poems in question, their drafts and variants, and other

58. Coleridge, *Collected Letters of Samuel Taylor Coleridge,* ed. Earl Leslie Griggs (Oxford, 1956–71), vol. 2, p. 1034.

59. Coleridge, *Biographia Literaria,* p. 271.

60. Ibid., p. 277.

61. McFarland, *Romanticism,* p. 78.

62. I question especially the statement that "to please his friend, Coleridge did for a while become, if not the 'most intense of Nature's worshippers', at least, as the 1850 version [of *The Prelude*] changes the expression to read, 'the most assiduous of her ministers'," (Ibid., p. 84)—a crude assessment belied by the author's own intricate analysis of his subject. More was involved in Coleridge's attitude to nature than pleasing Wordsworth.

63. Wordsworth's own summary statement of the matter is apparently correct, but minimal:

> Coleridge, my sister, and I, set off on a tour to Linton and other places in Devonshire; and in order to defray his part of the expense, Coleridge on the same afternoon commenced his poem of the Ancient Mariner, in which I was to have borne my part, and a few verses were written by me, and some assistance given in planning the poem; but our styles agreed so little, that I withdrew from the concern, and he finished it himself. (*Prose Works of William Wordsworth,* ed. W. J. B. Owen and Jane Worthington Smyser [Oxford, 1974], vol. 3, p. 374)

related matters.[64] The symbiosis of Coleridge and Wordsworth was such that to this day critics dispute which wrote some lines, stanzas, and entire poems. Coleridge displayed his amazing ability "to project himself into Wordsworth's style" and to compose lines that were "pure Wordsworth, both in their cadences and in their great Wordsworthian abstractions."[65]

But the relationship was not one-sided. Wordsworth also borrowed from Coleridge. More important,

> Coleridge's reliance on Wordsworth, though masochistic and psychically clinging, was not accompanied by reliance in the realm of thought. In that realm, indeed, the reliance was reversed. It is significant that Wordsworth never lost his enormous respect for his friend's mental powers, despite his growing disgust at Coleridge's weaknesses, despondency, and self-indulgence. If Coleridge was overwhelmed by Wordsworth, Wordsworth, in another way, was no less impressed by Coleridge.[66]

It was natural for Coleridge, always a voracious and omnivorous reader, dazzling intellectual, and persistent—perhaps compulsive—system builder to provide ideological leadership for his tremendously self-centered and largely isolated friend. But the closeness of the integration of the two was, again, surpassing. Jonathan Wordsworth wrote: "That Coleridge should have evolved a philosophical belief which Wordsworth assimilated is perhaps not very surprising. That he should also have been the first to portray the central Wordsworthian mystical experience is quite extraordinary,"[67] a feat which he accomplished in "Reflections on Entering into Active Life" printed in *Monthly Magazine* of October 1796 and in "This Lime-Tree Bower My Prison" of July 1797: "It is almost as if in 'This Lime-Tree Bower' Coleridge had deliberately taken one of Wordsworth's most recent poems—the Yew-tree lines—shown him how to make it fully Wordsworthian, and then decided not himself to compete."[68] Wordsworth, Coleridge was convinced, was to be the poet of the new dispensation, and he, Coleridge, its philosopher. For some eight or nine years (1796–1805) the two indeed proceeded to work together, as closely as was possible for two independent minds (in the opinion of Newton P. Stallknecht,[69] McFarland, Jonathan Wordsworth, and other specialists).

And during those years of cooperation—almost symbiosis—romanticism emerged in England. The usual focus on the publication of *Lyrical Ballads* in 1798 has been on the whole more appropriate than most other such specific and simple signposts in intellectual history. The first edition of *Lyrical Ballads*

64. McFarland, *Romanticism*, pp. 74–75.
65. Ibid., p. 60.
66. Ibid., p. 94.
67. J. Wordsworth, *Music of Humanity*, p. 193.
68. Ibid., p. 199.
69. Newton P. Stallknecht, *Strange Seas of Thought: Studies in William Wordsworth's Philosophy of Man and Nature,* (Bloomington, Ind., 1958), p. 141. (The first edition was published in 1945.)

opened with Coleridge's "Rime of the Ancyent Marinere" and, after twenty-one other pieces by the two poets, ended with Wordsworth's "Lines Written a Few Miles Above Tintern Abbey." More broadly considered, the years of cooperation encompassed almost all the outstanding contributions of William Wordsworth and Samuel Taylor Coleridge to English literature. That literature has not been the same since.

IV

Lyrical Ballads was accompanied and followed by other superb poems by Wordsworth and Coleridge. For Wordsworth, the height of poetic productivity might have come as late as the spring of 1802. Moorman presents the matter as follows:

> The spring of 1802 was a time of lyric creation never again equalled by Wordsworth. That is not to say that he never again wrote lyrics as great as those of this spring, for "The Solitary Reaper" and "I wandered lonely as a Cloud" and the rest of the "Ode" were yet to come, and several besides of a high order. Nor had he even reached the highest point of his creative activity, for *The Prelude* was yet unwritten save for the first two books, and so were all the sonnets. But the months from March to early June 1802 were unsurpassed for the frequency with which poem followed poem, as well as for their quality. In a period of about ten weeks he had written over thirty poems, nearly all of high, many of supreme, interest and excellence.[70]

But the creative élan did not last very long. It was succeeded by a rapid decline of poetic powers and, indeed, by the effective disappearance of Wordsworth as a great English poet, although he continued to live and write until 1850, became the official poet laureate of his country, and generally won rich recognition as a leading English man of letters. Those who strive for a more precise chronology date the break at some point in the time span 1802–7 inclusive—in any case roughly forty-five years before the poet's demise.[71]

The poetic collapse of Wordsworth was such that it, too, became a major problem in English literature, together with the emergence of romanticism and the nature and import of the stunning cooperation between Wordsworth and Coleridge. Lindenberger wrote, "A single and quite compelling question governs the argument behind much that is most admirable in modern Wordsworthian study: how are we to account for the brief flowering and rapid decline of the genius of one of our greatest poets?"[72] Mary Moorman tried to take common sense as far as it would go:

70. Moorman, *William Wordsworth,* p. 547.

71. Of the various specific dates proposed, I prefer the outside date of 1807, in part because of my very high regard for "The White Doe of Rylstone" written that year. In my estimate of that poem I follow Wordsworth himself and a minority of critics. See, esp., Danby, *Simple Wordsworth,* pp. 128–45. For a recent idiosyncratic assessment of Wordsworth's creativity see Clifford Siskin, *The Historicity of Romantic Discourse* (New York, 1988).

72. Herbert Lindenberger, *On Wordsworth's "Prelude"* (Princeton, 1963), p. ix.

The experience which he describes in the "Ode," the awareness of loss of vision, must have been of more recent occurrence; his full consciousness of it was, perhaps, not very much earlier than the actual writing of the "Rainbow" poem. To account for the change is another matter. It may be explicable perhaps in physical terms of the decline of his very acute "organic sensibility"—his extreme sensitivity to sights and sounds—as he approached middle life. For his visionary experience, as we have seen, was always the result of the perception of some event in the world of sense, such as the sight of the gibbet on Penrith Beacon, or the solitary climb to the eagle's eyrie, or an early morning walk around Esthwaite, or the cuckoo's cry. In boyhood his faculties of perception had led him naturally and almost inevitably over the border into the "visionary" world. That this now seldom happened may simply have been due to the gradual decline of these faculties into something less abnormally receptive. This process—perhaps itself natural and inevitable—may have been hastened by physical pain and weakness, from which he had suffered much during the last two or three years, and by the intensity with which he had laboured at his appointed task.[73]

McFarland continued his remarkable analysis of the interrelationship between Wordsworth and Coleridge by arguing that their separation meant the end of the creative period. In particular, Coleridge's departure for Malta in 1804 in search of health aborted his friend's work on his most important project, *The Recluse*, which was never to be completed. Wordsworth's "almost frantic" correspondence at the time revealed the extent of his dependency upon Coleridge's "'vast information', critical discernment, and philosophical understanding." As to Coleridge himself (for it is centrally important to keep in mind that Coleridge also stopped writing great poetry and that English literature lost not one but two great poets at about the same time), he had wrapped the poetic mantle around Wordsworth and had come to consider himself wholly inadequate as a poet in his own right. McFarland's exposition, relying on Coleridge's letters, deserves to be quoted at length:

> Thus Coleridge writes to Thelwall, on 17 December 1800: "As to Poetry, I have altogether abandoned it, being convinced that I never had the essentials of poetic Genius, and that I mistook a strong desire for original power." A letter to Godwin on 25 March 1801 makes it clear that self-comparison to Wordsworth precipitated this opinion:
>
> > The Poet is dead in me—my imagination . . . lies, like a Cold Snuff on the circular Rim of a Brass Candlestick. . . . If I die, and the Booksellers give you any thing for my Life, be sure to say—'Wordsworth descended on him, like the [Know Thyself] from Heaven; by shewing to him what true Poetry was, he made him know, that he himself was no Poet."
>
> Still again, on 29 July 1802 he writes to Southey: "As to myself, all my poetic Genius, if I ever really possessed any *Genius,* and it was not rather a mere general *aptitude* of Talent, and quickness in Imitation, is gone." To be

73. Moorman, William Wordsworth, p. 532.

sure, this last statement was written after Coleridge had begun the "Dejection Ode"; but that poem, as well as the lines "To William Wordsworth" of 1807, which seem to contradict his gloomy self-assessment, are both directly informed by Wordsworth's proximity. Besides these two poems, there is almost nothing further on in time that can be called poetic achievement.[74]

Whether one finds McFarland's explanation sufficient or not, the "symbiosis" of the two great poets and with it their creative magic belonged, indeed, to the past.[75]

Wordsworth not only stopped writing great poetry but also proceeded to rewrite and emasculate much of the great poetry he had already written. His constant changing of poems composed and often published earlier left a strange and depressing record in English literature. As Jonathan Wordsworth assessed the matter: "Wordsworth's revisions are normally—not always, but normally—for the worse; and this is true even at the period when in terms of

---

74. McFarland, *Romanticism*, pp. 97, 100–101; italics in original. McFarland's references are to Coleridge, *Collected Letters*, vol. 1, pp. 656, 714, 831. In another letter Coleridge wrote, "I abandon poetry altogether, I leave the higher and deeper Things to Wordsworth, the delightful popular and simply dignified to Southey; and reserve for myself the honourable attempt to make others feel and understand their writings, as they deserve to be felt and understood" (ibid., p. 623).

75. That past has been best preserved, of course, in the writings of the two men. To quote the second half of Wordsworth's "Stanzas Written in My Pocket-Copy of Thomson's 'Castle of Indolence'" (in his *Poems*, pp. 557–58):

> With him there often walked in friendly guise,
> Or lay upon the moss by brook or tree,
> A noticeable Man with large gray eyes,
> And a pale face that seemed undoubtedly
> As if a blooming face it ought to be;
> Heavy his low-hung lip did oft appear,
> Deprest by weight of musing Phantasy;
> Profound his forehead was, though not severe;
> Yet some did think that he had little business here,
>
> Sweet heaven forfend! his was a lawful right;
> Noisy he was, and gamesome as a boy;
> His limbs would toss about him with delight
> Like branches when strong winds the trees annoy.
> Nor lacked his calmer hours device or toy
> To banish listlessness and irksome care;
> He would have taught you how you might employ
> Yourself; and many did to him repair,—
> And certes not in vain; he had inventions rare.
>
> Expedients, too, of simplest sort he tried:
> Long blades of grass, plucked round him as he lay,
> Made, to his ear attentively applied,
> A pipe on which the wind would deftly play;
> Glasses he had, that little things display,
> The beetle panoplied in gems and gold,
> A mailèd angel on a battle-day;

original composition he is writing at his very best."[76] In a more specific context he wrote that "the bulk of Wordsworth's work is still read in reprints of the last edition of his lifetime. Most poems lose by this, but none loses more than 'The Ruined Cottage'."[77] Other critics used harsher words. Thus, F. W. Bateson wrote on the subject of *The Prelude,* the central example of persistent Wordsworthian emendation: "The 1850 revision is a deplorable affair. . . . On inspection [the changes] will almost always be found to be only superficial improvements—emptily elegant phrases, pretty-pretty images, pseudo-profundities."[78] In a similar vein he noted that "Wordsworth's later attempts to mitigate the social criticism in the version [of *The Prelude*] that he published in 1842 as 'Guilt and Sorrow' are almost comically ineffective."[79] Such far-reaching disparagements of the work of poetic revision of one of the most distinguished men of letters in the English language can be readily multiplied. As one follows Wordsworth in revision after revision (the poet produced some eleven or twelve versions of *The Prelude*) one becomes painfully aware not only of new infelicities and of a general weakening of tone and impact but also, time and again, of a loss—and indeed suppression—of the original vision.[80] The last issue will be addressed more directly in a later chapter.

In life, as in literature, Wordsworth proceeded to display an increasingly conservative—at times reactionary—stance. A "semi-atheist," as Coleridge described him early in their acquaintance, he became a pillar of the established church. Himself a visitor to revolutionary France and an enthusiastic supporter of the French Revolution, to the extent that he became suspect to the (admittedly stupid) British authorities, he turned definitely against new France around the year 1798 or a little later and moved steadily to the Right. For example, he was to be a determined opponent of the Reform Bill of 1832

> The mysteries that cups of flowers enfold,
> And all the gorgeous sights which fairies do behold.
>
> He would entice that other Man to hear
> His music, and to view his imagery;
> And, sooth, these two were each to the other dear:
> No livelier love in such a place could be:
> There did they dwell—from earthly labour free,
> As happy spirits as were ever seen;
> If but a bird, to keep them company,
> Or butterfly sate down, they were, I ween,
> As pleased as if the same had been a Maiden queen.

76. Wordsworth, *"Prelude 1799," 1805, 1850*, p. 567. See also pp. 565–84, Jonathan Wordsworth's "Two-Part Prelude of 1799."

77. J. Wordsworth, *Music of Humanity,* p. xiii.

78. Bateson, Wordsworth, p. 42 n. 1.

79. Ibid., p. 120.

80. I have not examined the Wordsworthian manuscript material—or, for that matter, the manuscript material of other major figures in this study. My evaluation is based on an extensive, but by no means exhaustive, study of published sources.

and a convinced advocate of capital punishment, which he championed in his
poetry. As Harper presented the matter with some indignation but also with
considerable insight:

> Up to a certain point he was guided by hope; later he was driven by fear. The
> two halves of his life are incongruous.
>
> The extent of the difference has never been fully appreciated, because it is
> not so perceptible in his poetry as it is in his letters and the reports of his
> conversation that have come down to us. A careful study, not only of what
> he said and wrote, but of what others said and wrote to him and about him,
> makes it quite clear that in the second half of his life he cursed what he once
> blessed, and blessed what he once cursed. The transition was fairly rapid,
> and it was complete. Moreover, it affected his poetry, affected not merely the
> subjects he chose and the general direction in which he turned his thoughts
> and feelings, but even the choice of words and the structure of his verse.[81]

When, late in his life, luminaries kept coming to his door to see the celebrated
man of letters or when he himself occasionally went out to pay visits, perhaps
the most appropriate pendant to the poet who had published *Lyrical Ballads* in
1798 was that other famous British writer, Sir Walter Scott, also a believer in
the true and unspoiled England, or Scotland—or, rather, the England, or
Scotland, that never was.

Coleridge's evolution broadly paralleled that of Wordsworth, although it
also contained, of course, unique Coleridgian characteristics. Like his former
associate, Coleridge kept changing his published works to make them more
conventional and unexceptionable.[82] Originally a radical supporter of the
French Revolution, he renounced his faith in revolutionary France in "France:
An Ode," published on April 16, 1798, after the French invasion of
Switzerland:

> Forgive me, Freedom! O forgive those dreams!
> I hear thy voice, I hear thy loud lament,
> From bleak Helvetia's icy caverns sent—

81. Harper, *William Wordsworth*, vol. 1, p. 6. Cf., e.g., Edward E. Bostetter, *The Romantic Ventriloquists: Wordsworth, Coleridge, Keats, Shelley, Byron* (Seattle, Wash., 1963), pp. 12–81, 308–13. My basic disagreement with Harper will become apparent in chapter 3. Another critic contrasted the two periods in the life of Wordsworth as follows: "You know that from 1797 to 1806 there was a real man there; you wonder whether behind the protective self-concern of the later years that man is still alive" (Willard L. Sperry, *Wordsworth's Anti-Climax* [New York, 1966], p. 224).

82. For instance, already in the second, 1800, edition of *Lyrical Ballads* there were such revisions in "The Rime of the Ancient Mariner" as replacing "And Christ would take no pity on" with "And never a saint took pity on" and "like God's own head" with "like an Angel's head." The last might well have been a response to a remark in the *British Critic* of October 1799: "The beginning of the second canto has much merit, if we except the very unwarrantable comparison to which no man can conceive: 'like God's own head', a simile which makes a reader shudder, not with poetic feeling, but with religious disapprobation" (Wordsworth and Coleridge, *Lyrical Ballads*, p. 324). Cf. B. R. McEldery, Jr., "Coleridge's Revision of 'The Ancient Mariner'," *Studies in Philology* 29(1932): 68–94.

I hear they groans upon her blood-stained streams!
Heroes, that for your peaceful country perished,
And ye that, fleeing, spot your mountain-snows
With bleeding wounds; forgive me, that I cherished
One thought that ever blessed your cruel foes![83]

Religion—unless one interprets as religion Wordsworth's all-absorbing vision—was always a more central (and also a more complex) issue for Coleridge than for Wordsworth. A son of a "sound" minister of the Church of England and a precocious and restless intellectual, Coleridge became an active Unitarian, as well as a political radical. Therefore, in contrast to Wordsworth, he had, as he moved right, to return to the established church and, in particular, to abandon the Unitarian dogma in favor of the conventional Trinitarian one, a process he accomplished by 1806. As to the role of religion in Coleridge's writing as a whole (not just on such explicitly religious compositions of his Unitarian period as his 1795 *Lectures on Revealed Religion, its Corruption, and its Political Views*), even "The Rime of the Ancient Mariner" has been interpreted as a fundamental defense of Christianity in an increasingly secular world.[84] Once the creative poetic outburst was over, religion, together with literary criticism, became the main subject of Coleridge's thought and writing. Moreover, in spite of constant illness, hypochondria, increasing opium addiction, and "failure ever to consolidate his thinking in any single, immediately coherent document"[85]—indeed, repeated failure to finish whatever he undertook—Coleridge achieved remarkable results. A specialist even credited Coleridge with creating "a new apologetics that ultimately he would use to transform Anglicanism and make it viable for another century."[86]

Coleridge's attraction to moral philosophy paralleled his general concentration on religion; and, again, it produced some striking results. In fact, the leading student of the subject writes that Coleridge's scattered writings

83. Coleridge, *Coleridge: Poetical Works,* p. 246.
84. It has been so interpreted notably by Jerome J. McGann, "The Meaning of the Ancient Mariner," *Critical Inquiry* 8, no. 1 (Autumn 1981): 35–67. This is certainly an extreme view. Note that McGann's elucidation of the poem as "salvation *of* Christ," rather than "salvation *in* Christ" (ibid., p. 54; italics in original) is very different from simply recognizing Christian—even dominant Christian—elements in "The Rime of the Ancient Mariner." McGann is also the author of an influential general study of romanticism, *The Romantic Ideology: A Critical Investigation* (Chicago, 1983).
85. Lawrence S. Lockridge, *Coleridge the Moralist* (Ithaca, N.Y., 1977), p. 17.
86. Elinor S. Shaffer, *"Kubla Khan" and "The Fall of Jerusalem": The Mythological School in Biblical Criticism and Secular Literature, 1770–1880* (New York, 1975), p. 26. By contrast, John Miller argued that by "privatizing" Christianity, Coleridge actually assisted the secularization which he was so ardently combatting ("Private Faith and Public Religion: S. T. Coleridge's Confrontation with Secularism," in *The Secular Mind,* ed. W. Warren Wagar (New York, 1982). For a more balanced general assessment of Coleridge as a religious thinker, see, e.g., Barth, *Coleridge and Christian Doctrine;* and for another accolade, see McFarland's statement, "I believe that Coleridge was the 'living link between religion and philosophy', for his own age" (*Coleridge and the Pantheist Tradition* [Oxford, 1962], p. 5; the internal quote reproduces Coleridge's opinion of Dante).

will show he was one of the great British moralists; though I will not argue
the matter, I suspect that in many ways he may have been the greatest. The
material I have collected is simply different in kind from that of any other
British moralist. It offers an uncommon density of argument and imaginative application of theory to moral situation, a richness of language, an
awareness of the close relationship of morality and psychology, and a sensitivity to moral ambiguity and evil.[87]

Still, during the last decades of Coleridge's life, it was his other preoccupation,
literary criticism, that probably eventually brought him most widespread and
lasting fame. In particular, Coleridge's *Biographia Literaria*—subjective, idiosyncratic, fragmentary, and disorganized but also deeply intelligent and brilliantly perceptive—has been repeatedly cited as a summit in its discipline. To
conclude, after his "symbiosis" with Wordsworth ended and until his death in
1834, Coleridge produced, in spite of all handicaps and obstacles, a considerable and highly important and influential body of work. But there was nothing
in that body resembling "The Rime of the Ancient Mariner" or "Kubla Khan."

Wordsworth and Coleridge's crucial loss of poetic vision and power was
linked to fear—indeed, terror. As I have already suggested, dread accompanied Coleridge throughout life. It found a particularly fertile soil in the
years and decades following his separation from Wordsworth.[88] The poet
himself gave the following painful description of his condition:

> It is a most instructive part of my Life . . . that I have been always preyed on
> by some Dread, and perhaps all my faulty actions have been the conse-
> quences of some Dread or other in my mind from fear of Pain, or Shame,
> not from prospect of Pleasure—so in my childhood and boyhood the horror
> of being detected with a sore head; afterwards imaginary fears of having the
> Itch in my Blood—than a short-lived Fit of Fears from sex—. . . . And
> finally stimulants in the fear and prevention of violent Bowel-attacks from
> mental agitation then almost epileptic night-horrors in my sleep and since
> then every error I have committed, has been the immediate effect of the
> Dread of these bad most shocking Dreams—any thing to prevent them.[89]

87. Lockridge, *Coleridge the Moralist*, p. 17. I also found useful such inclusive discussions of
Coleridge the philosopher as John H. Muirhead, *Coleridge as Philosopher* (London, 1930) and
Owen Barfield, *What Coleridge Thought* (Middletown, Conn., 1971). However, (as strikingly
illustrated by Barfield), they understandably tend to discuss his later, rather than earlier, thought
and to emphasize continuity, rather than breaks.

88. As an additional factor, it should be added that the renunciation of Unitarianism meant
for Coleridge an abandonment of certain optimistic assumptions and vistas and an affirmation or
reaffirmation of views such as the following in regard to original sin: "I believe most steadfastly
in original Sin; that from our mother's wombs our understandings are darkened; and even when
our understandings are in the Light, that our organization is depraved and our volitions imperfect" (quoted in Bate, Coleridge, p. 60). Cf. Bostetter, *Romantic Ventriloquists*, pp. 82–135, 313–
18.

89. Quoted in Bald, "Coleridge and 'The Ancient Mariner'" pp. 26–27.

Depression and dread were nowhere near as obvious in Wordsworth as in Coleridge, but there are nevertheless good reasons to suspect them in the author of *The Prelude*. Harper was probably correct in insisting that Wordsworth was driven by fear in the "second half" of his life. Such fear can be detected in the writer's constant changing of his published work, his extreme sensitivity to criticism (especially certain kinds), his eagerness to be both a part of and an all-out defender of the religious, social, and political establishment. On one occasion Wordsworth wrote that his *Prelude* (which he kept expurgating all his life) was to be to the projected *Recluse* as an antechapel to the main body of a Gothic church—except that he spelled the crucial word *Anti*-chapel despite his classical education in school and at Cambridge.[90] It was as if someone or something was pursuing Wordsworth every step of his way. Again, it was Coleridge who gave the best expression to their common predicament:

> Like one, that on a lonesome road
> Doth walk in fear and dread,
> And having once turned round walks on,
> And turns no more his head;
> Because he knows, a frightful fiend
> Doth close behind him tread.[91]

90. Wordsworth, *"Prelude" 1799, 1805, 1850*, p. 535.
91. Coleridge, *Coleridge: Poetical Works*, p. 203.

2

The Emergence of Romanticism in Germany

Die Lieb' ist frey gegeben,
Und keine Trennung mehr.
Es wogt das volle Leben
Wie ein unendlich Meer,
Nur eine Nacht der Wonne—
Ein ewiges Gedicht—
Und unser aller Sonne
Ist Gottes Angesicht.

Love is freely given,
Separation is no more.
Full life rolls on
Like an endless sea.
Only one night of ecstasy—
An eternal poem—
And the sun for all of us
Is the countenance of God.

NOVALIS,
from *Hymnen an die Nacht*

During the very years when Wordsworth and Coleridge were introducing romanticism into English literature, Friedrich von Hardenberg (1772–1801), to be known as Novalis, was bringing it into German poetry and prose.

Wie ein König
Der irdischen Natur
Ruft es jede Kraft

41

Zu Zahllosen Verwandlungen
Und seine Gengenwart allein
Offenbart die Wunderherrlichkeit
Des irdischen Reichs.
Abwarts wend ich mich
Zu der heiligen, unaussprechlichen
Geheimnisvollen Nacht—
Fernab liegt die Welt,
Wie versenkt in eine tiefe Gruft
Wie wüst und einsam
Ihre Stelle![1]

As a king
Of worldly nature
It calls each power
To countless changes
And its presence alone
Bares the wondrous splendor
Of the earth's kingdom.
Downwards I turn
To the holy, unspeakable
The mysterious Night—
Over there, far, lies the world,
As if sunken in a deep vault,
How wasted and lonely
Her place![2]

O! sauge, Geliebter,
Gewaltig mich an,
Dass ich entschlummern
Und lieben kann.
Ich fühle des Todes
Verjungende Flut,
Zu Balsam und Aether
Verwandelt mein Blut—
Ich lebe bey Tage
Voll Glauben und Muth
Und sterbe die Nächte
In heiliger Glut.[3]

1. *Hymnen an die Nacht,* in *Novalis,* ed. Richard Samuel and Hans-Joachim Mähl (Munich, 1978), vol. 1, p. 148 (Unless otherwise indicated, translations from the German are Theodore R. Weeks' and mine, with the final responsibility resting with me.) For a rhymed English translation see *Hymns to the Night,* trans. Mabel Cotterell (London, 1948).
2. *Hymns to the Night,* trans. Richard C. Higgins, 3d ed. (New York, 1988), 49.
3. *Hymnen,* p. 159.

Oh engulf me, my love,
Violently
That I may fall into eternal slumber
And love,
I feel death's
Rejuvenating flood,
My blood transformed
Into balsam and ether—
By day I live   .
Full of faith and courage
And die at night
In holy ardor.

Gehoben ist der Stein—
Die Menschheit ist erstanden—
Wir alle bleiben dein
Und fühlen keine Banden.
Der herbste Kummer fleucht
Vor deiner goldnen Schaale,
Wenn Erd und Leben weicht
Im letzten Abendmahle.[4]

The Stone is lifted—
Humanity is risen—
We all remain yours
And feel no chains.
The sharpest care flies off
Before your golden basin,
When earth and life give way
At the last supper.[5]

Der Jüngling bist du, der seit langer Zeit
Auf unsern Gräbern steht in tiefen Sinnen;
Ein tröstlich Zeichen in der Dunkelheit—
Der höhern Menschheit freudigen Beginnen.
Was uns gesenkt in tiefe Traurigkeit
Zieht uns mit süsser Sehnsucht nun von hinnen.
Im Tode war das ewge Leben kund,
Du bist der Tod und machst uns erst gesund.[6]

4. Ibid., p. 170.
5. *Hymns,* trans. Higgins, p. 33.
6. *Hymnen,* p. 167.

You're the youth since ancient days
Has stood in contemplation of our graves:
A comforting sign in the darkness—
A hopeful start to our new humanity.
What sank us in our deepest down despair
Draws us from here now with sweet craving.
In death eternal life is made known,
And you are Death who makes us whole at last.[7]

Gelobt sei uns die ewge Nacht,
Gelobt der ewge Schlummer.
Wohl hat der Tag uns warm gemacht,
Und welk der lange Kummer.
Die Lust der Fremde ging uns aus,
Zum Vater wollen wir nach Haus.[8]

Blessed be the endless Night to us,
Blessed the endless sleep.
Truly the day has made us hot,
And long care's withered us.
The wish for strange things is gone away,
And now we want our Father's home.[9]

Was passt, das muss sich ründen,
Was sich versteht, sich finden,
Was gut ist, sich verbinden,
Was liebt, zusammenseyn.
Was hindert, muss entweichen,
Was krumm ist, muss sich gleichen,
Was fern ist, sich erreichen,
Was keimt, das muss gedeihn.[10]

What fits must become round
What is understood must be found,
What is good, must connect,
What loves, must be together.
What hinders, must let go,
What is crooked, must be straightened,

---

7. *Hymns*, trans. Higgins, p. 31.
8. *Hymnen*, p. 175. This last section (pp. 175–77) carries the heading "Sehnsucht nach dem Tode" (Longing for Death).
9. As rendered in *Hymns*, trans. Higgins, p. 39.
10. From "An Adolf Selmnitz" (To Adolf Selmnitz) in *Novalis*, vol. 1, p. 109.

What is far, must be reached,
What sprouts, that must flourish.

Soll ich getrennt seyn ewig?—ist Vorgefühl
Der künftigen Vereinigung, dessen, was
    Wir hier für Unser schon erkannten,
Aber nicht ganz noch besitzen konnten—

Ist dies auch Rausch? so bliebe der Nüchternheit,
Der Wahrheit nur die Masse, der Thon, und das
    Gefühl der Leere, des Verlustes
Und der vernichtigenden Entsagung.[11]

Must I be eternally alienated?—is this not presentiment
Of the future union, of that, which
Already here we recognize as our own,
But are as yet unable to possess entirely—

Is this too intoxication?—so let remain of soberness,
Of truth only the substance, the sound, and the
Feeling of emptiness, of loss
And of destroying abnegation.

Uns barg der Wald vor Sonnenschein.
Das ist der Frühling fiel mir ein.
Kurz um, ich sah, dass jetzt auf Erden
Die Menschen sollten Götter werden.
Nun wusst ich wohl, wie mir geschah
Und wie das wurde was ich sah.[12]

The wood hid us from sunshine.
This is spring! I thought;
And shortly, I saw, that now on earth
Men must become Gods.
Now I knew well, what was happening to me,
And how that which I saw came to be.

Especially in the case of Novalis, prose was often very close to poetry, whether as regards particular statements or entire larger pieces.

We seek everywhere the limitless and find only limits.[13]

11. From "Anfang," (Beginning), in *Novalis*, p. 110.
12. *Novalis*, vol. 1, p. 140.
13. From "Blüthenstaub" ("Pollen" or "Flower Dust") in *Novalis*, vol. 2, p. 227. The original German reads, "Wir suchen überall das Unbedingte, und finden immer nur Dinge."

Life is the beginning of death. Life exists for the sake of death. Death is simultaneously ending and beginning, division and closer bonding. Through death, reduction is completed.[14]

Much is too tender to be thought, let alone to be spoken.[15]

We are on a mission: we are called to create the world.[16]

Turning to *The Novices of Sais,* we read:[17]

Various are the roads of man. He who follows and compares them will see strange figures emerge, figures which seem to belong to that great cipher which we discern written everywhere, in wings, eggshells, clouds and snow, in crystals and in stone formations, on ice-covered waters, on the inside and outside of mountains, of plants, beasts and men, in the lights of heaven, on scored disks of pitch or glass or in iron filings round a magnet, and in strange conjunctures of chance. In them we suspect a key to the magic writing, even a grammar, but our surmise takes on no definite forms and seems unwilling to become a higher key. It is as though an alkahest has been poured over the senses of man. Only at moments do their desires and thoughts seem to solidify. Thus arise their presentiments, but after a short time everything swims again before their eyes.[18]

Everything leads me back into myself.[19]

[The teacher] wants us rather to go our own way, because every new road goes through new countries and each in the end leads anew to these dwellings, to this sacred home. I, too, then will inscribe my figure, and if according to the inscription, no mortal can lift the veil, we must seek to become immortal; he who does not seek to lift it, is no true novice of Sais.[20]

It must have been a long time before men thought of giving a common name to the manifold objects of their senses, and of placing themselves in opposition to them. Through practice developments were furthered, and in all developments occur separations and divisions that may well be compared with the splitting of a ray of light. It was only gradually that our inwardness split into such various forces, and with continued practice this splitting will increase.[21]

---

14. Ibid., p. 231.
15. Ibid., p. 237.
16. Ibid., p. 241.
17. *Novalis,* vol. 1, pp. 199–236. I am also using, for its English, *The Novices of Sais,* Trans. Ralph Manheim (New York, 1949).
18. *Novices of Sais,* pp. 3–5.
19. Ibid., p. 13.
20. Ibid., p. 17.
21. Ibid., p. 19.

When we read and hear true poems, we feel the movement of nature's inner reason, and like its celestial embodiment, we dwell in it and hover over it at once. Scientists and poets have, by speaking *one* language, always shown themselves to be *one* people. What the scientists have gathered and arranged in huge, well-ordered stores, has been made by the poets into the daily food and consolation of human hearts; the poets have broken up the one, great, immeasurable nature and moulded it into various small amenable natures. . . . Those who would know her spirit truly must therefore seek it in the company of poets, where she is free and pours forth her wondrous heart.[22]

Soon nature learned friendlier ways again, she became gentler and more amiable, more prone to favor the desires of man. Little by little her heart learned human emotions, her fantasies became more joyful, she became companionable, responding gladly to the friendly questioner, and thus little by little she seems to have brought back the old golden age, in which she was man's friend, consoler, priestess and enchantress, when she lived among men and divine association made men immortal. Then once more the constellations will visit the earth that they looked upon so angrily in those days of darkness; then the sun will lay down her harsh scepter, becoming again a star among stars, and all the races of the world will come together after long separation. Families orphaned of old will be reunited, and each day will see new greetings, new embraces; then the former inhabitants of the earth will return, on every hill embers will be rekindled; everywhere the flames of life will blaze up, old dwelling places will be rebuilt, old times renewed, and history will become the dream of an infinite, everlasting present.[23]

Attentiveness to subtle signs and traits, an inward poetic life, practiced senses, a simple, God-fearing heart—these are the basic requisites for a true friend of nature, and without them his striving will not prosper.[24]

The epitome of what stirs our feeling is called nature, hence nature stands in an immediate relation to the functions of our body that we call senses. Unknown and mysterious relations within our body cause us to surmise unknown and mysterious states in nature; nature is a community of the marvelous into which we are initiated by our body, and which we learn to know in the measure of our body's faculties and abilities.[25]

"Only the poets have felt what nature can be to mankind," began a handsome youth, "and in this connection it can once more be said that the humanity in them is in the most perfect diffusion, and that consequently through their mirrored clarity and mobility each impression is communicated on all sides in its infinite variations. They find everything in nature. To

22. Ibid., pp. 25–27; italics in original.
23. Ibid., pp. 33–35.
24. Ibid., p. 37.
25. Ibid., p. 77.

them alone its soul remains no stranger, and not in vain do they seek all the ecstasies of the golden age in its presence. For them nature has all the variety of an infinite soul, and more than the cleverest, most alive of men, it astounds us with ingenious turns and fancies, with correspondences and deviations, with grandiose ideas and trifling whimsies. So inexhaustible is nature's fantasy, that no one will seek its company in vain. It has power to beautify, animate, confirm, and even though an unconscious, unmeaning mechanism seems to govern the part, the eye that looks deeper discerns a wonderful sympathy with the human heart in concurrences and in the sequence of isolated accidents. The wind is a movement of the air; it can spring from various outward causes, but is it not more to the lonely, yearning heart when it comes murmuring, blowing from places beloved, when with a thousand dark, melancholy sounds it seems to melt a silent grief into a deep, melodious sigh? And in the youthful, unassuming green of meadows in spring, does the young lover not see his whole flowery heart expressed with enchanting truth? And has the luxuriance of a spirit seeking contentment in wine, ever appeared with greater joy and vigor than in a glistening, full-blown cluster of grapes, hiding amid broad leaves? Poets are accused of exaggeration and at best forgiven for their unreal images; without looking closer, people ascribe to poets' fancy the miraculous nature that sees and hears things which others do not hear and see, whose tender madness governs the real world at will; but to me it seems that the poets do not exaggerate nearly enough, since they content themselves with darkly surmising the magic of nature's language and with playing on fancy as a child might play with his father' magic wand. They do not know what forces they have as vassals, what worlds are bound to obey them. Is it not true that stones and woods are obedient to music, that under the spell of music they serve man's will like house-pets?—Is it not true that the loveliest flowers bloom for the beloved, and delight in adorning her? Does the sky not grow blue for her and the sea turn smooth?—Is it not true that all nature, as well as face and gesture, color and pulse, expresses the emotion of each one of the wonderful higher beings we call men? Does the cliff not become a unique Thou, whenever I speak of it? And what am I but the stream, when I look sadly down into its waters and lose my thoughts in its flow? Only a tranquil sensuous spirit will understand the world of plants, only a high-spirited child or a savage will understand beasts.—Whether anyone has ever understood the stones and the stars, I do not know, but if so, he must surely have been a noble creature. Only those statues that have come down to us from a lost age of mankind's glory, are illuminated by so deep a spirit, so rare an understanding of the stone world; they cover the sensitive beholder with a rind of stone that seems to grow inward. The sublime has power to petrify, hence we should not be surprised at the sublime in nature or its influence, or fail to know where to seek it. Might nature not have turned to stone at the sight of God? Or from fear at the advent of man?"[26]

"Whose heart does not leap with joy," cried the youth with glittering eye, "when the innermost life of nature invades him in all its fullness! When the

26. Ibid., pp. 85–91.

overpowering emotion for which language has no other name than love, expands within him like an all-dissolving vapor and, trembling with sweet fear, he sinks into the dark, alluring heart of nature, consumes his poor personality in the crashing waves of lust, and nothing remains but a focus of infinite procreative forces, a yawning vortex in an immense ocean? What is the flame that is manifested everywhere? A fervent embrace, whose sweet fruits fall like sensuous dew. Water, firstborn child of airy fusions, cannot deny its voluptuous origin and reveals itself an element of love, and of its mixture with divine omnipotence on earth. Not without truth have ancient sages sought the origin of things in water, and indeed, they spoke of water more exalted than sea and well water. A water in which only primal fluidity is manifested, as it is manifested in liquid metal; therefore should men revere it always as divine. How few up to now have immersed themselves in the mysteries of fluidity, and there are some in whose drunken soul this surmise of the highest enjoyment and the highest life has never wakened. In thirst this world soul is revealed, this immense longing for liquefaction. The intoxicated feel only too well the celestial delight of the liquid element, and ultimately all pleasant sensations are multiform flowings and stirrings of those primeval waters in us. Even sleep is nothing but the high tide of that invisible world sea, and waking is the ebb tide. How many men stand by the rivers that make drunk and fail to hear the lullaby of the motherly waters or to enjoy the entrancing play of their never-ending waves! In the golden age we lived like these waves; in variegated clouds, those floating seas and springs of life on earth, the generations of mankind loved and procreated in never-ending games, they were visited by the children of heaven, and only in that great event which holy sagas call the deluge, was this flowering world submerged; a hostile being hurled down the earth, and a few men were left in the alien world, washed up on the crags of the new mountains."[27]

No one will fathom nature who possesses no sense of nature, no inward organ for creating and dividing nature, who does not, as though spontaneously recognize and distinguish nature everywhere, who does not with an inborn creative joy, a rich and fervent kinship with all things, mingle with all of nature's creatures through the medium of feeling, who does not feel his way into them. He who has a sound and practiced sense of nature enjoys nature by studying it, and takes delight in infinite variety, its inexhaustible joy, and has no need to be disturbed in his pleasures by useless words. It seems to him rather that a man cannot be too much alone with nature, cannot speak of her tenderly enough, cannot be attentive and undisturbed enough in his contemplation of her. In nature he feels as though in the arms of his chaste bride, and only to her does he confide the intuitions to which he has attained in sweet hours of intimacy. Happy I call this son, this darling of nature, whom she permits to behold her in her duality, as a power that engenders and bears, and in her unity, as an endless, everlasting marriage. His life will be a plenitude of all pleasures, a voluptuous chain, and his religion will be the real, the true naturalism.[28]

27. Ibid., pp. 103–7.
28. Ibid., pp. 109–11.

In the case of Novalis, as with Wordsworth and Coleridge, there were preliminary stages—and perhaps deviations—before the poet could express his vision and impose it on world literature. It is noteworthy that Novalis, too, experienced a more "rational" and "enlightened" period before turning to what has been best described as *magischer Idealismus* (magical idealism) and, indeed, a form of mysticism. There were important influences, especially those of Fichte and Hemsterhuis,[29] as well as of the poet's immediate environment. One scholar gives the following capsule description of that environment at the time when Novalis was emerging as a major poet:

> [Novalis's important works] came in considerable degree prompted by close association with the group of young theoreticians of Romanticism that met frequently, especially through the year 1798, in the home of August Wilhelm Schlegel in Jena. There, around the supper table convened the urbane host, his immensely gifted and somewhat erratic brother Friedrich, their authoress wives, and a varying combination of intellectual visitors which included the poet Tieck, the theologian Schleiermacher, the scientist Steffens, and, on rare occasions, Goethe. From those memorable suppers and evenings the vivid mind of Novalis absorbed Friedrich Schlegel's brilliant and iconoclastic ideas about the nature of history, science, philosophy, art, and morals. From August Wilhelm Schlegel he heard notions of great programs of application of Friedrich's ideas to contemporary literature and society. From all of them he heard of the bankruptcy of eighteenth century rationalism and the inevitable approaching triumph of the new poetry of the intuitive heart.[30]

There struck also, on March 19, 1797, the shattering death of Novalis' very young fiancée, Sophie von Kühn, generally considered by specialists as the central event in the poet's biography, especially in his creative life.[31]

Although Novalis was a writer for only ten years and an important writer for no longer than the last three or four years of that decade, there is an abundance of analyses, periodizations, and classifications of his work. Thus, the poet's admiring biographer Friedrich Hiebel emphasized that in the three years separating Sophie von Kühn's death and his own terminal illness, Novalis went through three stages, always deepening his creative perception: he responded primarily as a thinker during the first year, increasingly as a poet during the second, and combined these two aspects of his genius by means of Christian mysticism in the third.[32] Soviet specialist in German

29. See, esp., Hans-Joachim Mähl, *Die Idee des goldenen Zeitalters im Werk des Novalis* (Heidelberg, 1965).

30. Novalis, *"Hymns to the Night" and Other Selected Writings*, trans. Charles E. Passage (New York, 1960), pp. viii–ix.

31. As Novalis wrote and underlined in his diary, "Xstus und Sophie" (Christ and Sophie), and "Ich habe zu Söpchen Religion—nicht Liebe" (I have for dear little Sophie religion—not love) (Friedrich Hiebel, *Novalis: deutscher Dichter, europäischer Denker, christlicher Seher*, 2d rev. ed. [Bern 1972], pp. 68, 70.

32. Ibid., p. 9.

romanticism R. M. Gabitova analyzed Novalis' works in regard to the golden age which they heralded. She concluded that the golden age was presented as the interpenetration and merging of man and nature in *Die Lehrlinge zu Sais,* a reborn and renewed Christianity in *Die Christenheit oder Europa* (Christianity or Europe), the Kingdom of God in *Hymnen an die Nacht* and *Geistliche Lieder* (Spiritual Songs), an idealized family monarchy in *Glauben und Liebe* (Faith and Love), and permeation of the world with poetry in *Heinrich von Ofterdingen.*[33] But although these and other such divisions and classifications can be helpful, they should not be allowed to obscure the singular core of Novalis' romantic vision.

In fact, many commentators have noted that man and nature, the two main themes of Novalis' creativity, tended, in his case, to become one. The fundamental and ideal identity of the human being and nature produced living, or spiritual, nature and "natural man," that is, man merged with nature. Humanity moved from the original golden age, when man and nature were one, to a period of a deplorable separation and then to the third stage of a triumphant reunification and a new and golden age, even more golden for its having overcome and absorbed the period of division. God, love, poetry, and the night represented the same overwhelming organic synthesis. Poetry, to repeat, constituted the special bond between man and nature; and it was the poets who, through their intuitive feeling, served as the true glue of the universe. As in the pieces by Wordsworth and Coleridge, water and wind coursed through the creations of Novalis, including the remarkable identification of water, love, and basic reality in the penultimate prose selection.

Death, too, was an avatar of Novalis's fundamental vision. Probably the most celebrated poet of death in world literature, Novalis saw death as the purpose of life and the ultimate expression of that transcendent unity which remained always his one passion. Championed by Kleist and others, the cult of death was to play a notable role in German romanticism.[34] Perhaps even more interestingly, death can be discovered at the emergence of English romanticism, as well as German. Thus, Frances Ferguson emphasized that Wordsworth's discussions of language remained conspicuously tied to one central metaphor, that of the epitaph or tombstone:[35]

---

33. Rimma M. Gabitova, *Filosofiia nemetskogo romantizma* (Moscow, 1978), p. 252.

34. See, esp., Walter Rehm, *Orpheus, der Dichter und die Toten: Selbstdeutung und Totenkult bei Novalis–Hölderlin–Kleist* (Düsseldorf, 1950). The first part of this large volume deals with Novalis. The presentation is extremely interesting and useful, although insufficiently critical and determined to fit Novalis neatly into the Christian framework. As to my larger point of a certain interchangeability of key elements of Novalis' vision, this phenomenon has been recognized in different ways by numerous commentators. For instance, Hermann A. Korff wrote: "All four kingdoms of the blue flower, the kingdom of secret nature, the kingdom of the night, the kingdom of Christ, and the kingdom of poetry—they are all in their deepest essence the same. They are four transformations of a single spiritual substance" (*Geist der Goethezeit-Versuch einer idealen Entwicklung der klassisch–romantischen Literaturgeschichte,* vol. 3 [Leipzig, 1957], p. 55).

35. Frances Ferguson, *Wordsworth: Language as Counter-Spirit* (New Haven, Conn., 1977), p. ii.

When the imagery becomes most strongly organic in Wordsworth's poetry
(as in the Lucy poems with all their flowers), one invariably finds it linked
with the epitaph and its inorganic counterpart, the tombstone.[36]

Funeral monuments seem in Wordsworth's discourse, almost to be the
first poetry.[37] Language and death are indissolubly related from the beginning of language in both the pre-alphabetic signs of funeral monuments and
in the alphabetic inscriptions which reinforce the signs which the monuments themselves are.[38]

Lyrical Ballads itself was to a remarkable extent about death. One analysis
indicates that of the twenty-three pieces published in the first edition, ten had
death as their main subject, another three had it as an important topic, and
only ten were not obviously concerned with it.[39] If, according to Novalis, it
was a task of poets to link the living and the dead, English romantic poets
performed that task as much as German ones.

Novalis' passion for unity, merging, and absorption meant turning inward. Many commentators have noted that his creative spirit (and perhaps the
creative spirit of romanticism in general) moved typically in a circle, returning to the starting point. Within that frame of reference, going away could
not be easily distinguished from coming back or even leaving from entering.
In another sense, however, progression meant for Novalis penetrating to the
deeper inner reality, beyond the outer layers, under the veil: "Everything
leads me back into myself." Werner Kohlschmidt made a fascinating analysis
of the central vocabulary of that process: *inner, innerlich, die Innerlichkeit, innig,
die Innigkeit, das Innere, innerste,* and so on ("inner" in the positive, comparative, and superlative forms; "innerness"; and other cognate words, often
not readily translatable into English).[40] After the death of Sophie, in particular, *inner* became a key and constantly repeated term for the hoped-for true
and complete reunion, "das Verlangen nach innigerer, gänzlicher Ver-
mischung" ("the desire for *inniger,* total merger").[41] *Und keine Trennung mehr.*
Novalis wrote in *Heinrich von Ofterdingen:* "Imagination represents the after-
life either on high or in the depths or in metempsychosis. We dream of
journeys through the universe, but is the universe not within us? We do not
realize the profundities of our spirits. Inward is the direction of the mystic
path. Within us or nowhere is eternity with its worlds of past and future."[42]
One scholar wrote, "Of the great German romantic poets, Novalis is the

36. Ibid., p. xii.

37. Ibid., p. 29.

38. Ibid., p. 30. For another incisive treatment of the issue of Wordsworth and death, see
David Ferry, *The Limits of Mortality: An Essay on Wordsworth's Major Poems* (Middletown, Conn.,
1959), esp. pp. 83–89.

39. I want to thank my wife, Arlene Riasanovsky, for this analysis.

40. Werner Kohlschmidt, "Der Wortschatz der Innerlichkeit bei Novalis," in *Festschrift Paul
Kluckhohn und Hermann Schneider gewidmet zu ihrem 60. Geburtstag* (Tübingen, 1948), esp. p. 398.

41. Ibid., p. 420.

42. Translation from Novalis, *Hymns,* ed. Passage, p. 66. The emphasis on "inner" experience had been propounded in Germany by Pietism, especially.

most problematic, not because he is less, but because he is *more* romantic than the others, because he approaches more closely to the ideal of Romanticism."[43]

As in the case of Wordsworth, being "more romantic" included the element of solipsism. If the English poet was accused by Coleridge and others of the inability to dramatize anyone but himself in his works, his German contemporary usually did not even have any characters so to dramatize. And even when present, they had the disconcerting ability to lose independent existence. To refer to the celebrated story of Hyacinth and Roseblossom, as presented and discussed by Jack Forstman:

> The fulfillment is a return to the beginning. The form hidden by the veil is Roseblossom, and he is reunited with her; but the new unity is richer than the original one. At the beginning they lived together in innocent harmony; now their full union is consummated. What he sought was what he had in the beginning; what he found was the earlier state raised to a higher power. In a variant to the ending of this fable Novalis writes: "He lifted the veil of the goddess of Sais—but what did he see? He saw—wonder of wonders— himself." It is all the same. Roseblossom is himself, from whom he has been alienated and to whom he has now returned. The vision of Novalis is the vision of movement from unity to separation to new unity; his is the Song of Return.[44]

In their personal lives, too, Novalis and Wordsworth had much more in common than was immediately apparent. Although their biographies were in many respects different,[45] both were possessed by an overpowering and remarkably similar vision. Whereas there is no way to measure precisely and compare Wordsworth's spots of time and absorption into nature to Novalis's ecstatic merger with nature or night or love, the similarities are striking. The response to nature was not primarily intellectual; in fact, in a sense it was anti-intellectual. It depended on feeling, intuition, a simple and direct perception of the living wholeness of being. Novalis tried to explain the matter in a passage that would have been congenial to Wordsworth:

> No one can tell how long it will take a man to learn nature's secrets. Some fortunates have attained this knowledge early, some in advanced old age. A true inquirer never grows old, every eternal yearning lies outside the term of life, and the more the outer husk fades, the brighter, clearer and richer grows the kernel. Nor does this gift attach to outward beauty or strength or intelligence or any human quality. In every walk of life, among all ages and races,

---

43. Alan Menhennet, *The Romantic Movement* (Totowa, N.J., 1981), p. 37; italics in original.

44. Jack Forstman, *Romantic Triangle: Schleiermacher and Early German Romanticism* (Missoula, Mont., 1977), p. 48. Irving Babbitt was among those who made the same point earlier (*Rousseau and Romanticism* [Boston, 1991], p. 226).

45. For an insistent—indeed, excessive—linking of the details of Novalis' life with his creative work, see Heinz Ritter, *Der unbekannte Novalis: Friedrich von Hardenberg im Spiegel seiner Dichtung* (Göttingen, 1967).

in all epochs and under every reach of heaven, there have been men selected
by nature as her favorites, and endowed with inner conception. Often these
men seemed simpler and more awkward than others and spent their whole
life covered by the darkness of the herd. Indeed it is a great rarity to find true
understanding of nature accompanied by great eloquence, cleverness and a
noble bearing, since commonly it goes hand in hand with simple words, an
upright mind, and an unassuming character. This sense seems to develop
most easily and frequently in the workshops of artisans and artists, and in
those occupations such as farming, seafaring, cattle-breeding, mining, in
which men are in constant contact and struggle with nature.[46]

But it was the true poets who provided the real link between humanity and
nature—indeed, were absorbed into nature. The maternal, nuptial, engulfing
quality of the relationship was possibly even more pronounced in Novalis
than in Wordsworth. So was, perhaps, the superior, even supreme, role assigned to poetry and poets in the cosmic order. Poets were intrinsically
related to priests; in fact, they were the priests of the new dispensation. It can
also be argued that Novalis was more explicit, more dogmatic, more verbal,
and more shrill than Wordsworth; but these are hardly major distinctions,
because Wordsworth was explicit and dogmatic enough and his words among
the most memorable in the English language.

Rather, the difference was in the ending. Wordsworth repudiated his vision, and spent long decades expurgating and repressing it. Novalis persisted
in his and died in its magical, or mystic, blaze before he reached the age of
twenty-nine—died not only with his vision intact (some would say) but
because of it.[47]

II

As indicated earlier, Novalis was not alone in his romantic search and creation
in Germany. A slight chronological priority may even be assigned to Wilhelm
Heinrich Wackenroder (1773–98), who published in 1797, together with Ludwig Tieck, *Herzensergiessungen eines kunstliebenden Klosterbruders* (Outpour-
ings of the Heart of an Art-loving Cloister Brother). That piece, together
with his part of the *Phantasien über die Kunst für Freunde der Kunst* (Phantasies
About Art for Friends of Art), which came out posthumously in 1799, as-

46. Novalis, *Novices of Sais,* pp. 117–19.
47. Discussions of Novalis's health and physical condition tend to resemble similar discussions concerning Coleridge and to focus on the same issue—how the poet's condition relates to
his creativity. Attempts have been made to present Novalis as a fundamentally healthy and
balanced individual. At the other extreme, such a scholar as Gerhard Schulz suggested venereal
disease and impotence (*Novalis in Selbstzeugnissen und Bilddokumenten* [Hamburg, 1969], p. 109).
The issue is complicated by our insufficient knowledge of tuberculosis, the illness which killed
Novalis and became the quintessential disease of romanticism.

sured Wackenroder a seminal role in the emergence and development of romanticism.[48]

The *Herzensergiessungen* contained, in effect, two parts. In the first the authors created, on the basis of Vasari and some other sources but also following their own imagination, an ideal world of art and artists featuring "divine Raphael," Leonardo da Vinci, Michelangelo, and Dürer, as well as some lesser figures. Art was essentially a heavenly miracle. Artistic genius could not be taught or learned, and Raphael did not know why he painted as he did. Or, according to one story, his perfect Madonnas resulted from a nighttime visitation from the original, transforming his inadequate effort on the canvas into the ideal, which he proceeded to reproduce to the end of his life. The second part addressed music and raised it in turn to the position of the supreme and absolute art; but this part also contained at the end the story of its musical hero's misery in a totally unmusical world.

Art and music were very closely related in Wackenroder's work to God, which explains the positive and radiant tone in his depiction of them.[49] Moreover, in contrast to Friedrich Schlegel and Tieck, his aim was not to aestheticize religion—not to turn religion into art—but to find religion in art, to raise art to the level of religion.[50] Again, as in the case of Novalis, we are at the threshold of a *magische,* mystical transformation. Admiring a noble work of art meant praying. Great painting blended with ethical or religious perfection. Music contained the original speech of man, which he had to learn again if he was to regain paradise and be absorbed by the infinite.[51] Art stood out as "the higher lover" of the artist, his "religious love" or "beloved religion." Nature, too, was of first importance. Together with art it represented the two main revelations of God; and it was the direct revelation, whereas art proceeded through the artist.

Alexander Gillies insisted that *Herzensergiessungen*

> founded Romanticism without knowing it. Its views on art and music, its medievalism, its tender yearning for a world of wonder, religion, and creative universality, and its rapturous emotion let loose the most powerful currents in the writing of later poets and critics. Its every page is coloured by

48. I am using the German texts as published in Wilhelm Heinrich Wackenroder and Ludwig Tieck, *"Herzensergiessungen eines kunstliebenden Klösterbruders" together with Wackenroder's contribution to the "Phantasien über die Kunst für Freunde der Kunst,"* ed. Alexander Gillies (Oxford, 1948).

49. That radiance was a hallmark of Wackenroder. Major difficulties arose, however, in combining art and life, the tragic leitmotif of the writer's own biography. Music signified escape from the suffering and the obligations of the surrounding world. Wackenroder even declared, "Art is a seductive forbidden fruit; he who tastes its innermost sweetest sap once is irretrievably lost for the daily practical world" (Wackenroder and Tieck, *Herzensergiessungen,* p. 153). As in the case of Novalis, Wackenroder's vision was not of this earth.

50. Gerhard Fricke, "Bemerkungen zu Wilhelm Heinrich Wackenroders Religion der Kunst," in *Festschrift Paul Kluckhohn,* esp. p. 353.

51. On this last point, see Walter Silz, *Early German Romanticism: Its Founders and Heinrich von Kleist* (Cambridge, Mass., 1929), p. 198.

the *mal du siècle*—and in a form far more subtly effective than the titanic agonies usually associated with this disease.[52]

The medieval studies of Wackenroder led to Tieck's edition of the *Minnesänger*, as well as to his interest in the *Märchen* and the folk-story already noted; from Tieck there is a direct line to Savigny and the brothers Grimm on the one hand and to Novalis' *Heinrich von Ofterdingen* on the other.[53]

It is noteworthy that Wackenroder achieved his results without the aid, so far as we know, of the philosophy an theory of Romanticism that were developed concurrently with his career. . . . Wackenroder's work was an independent growth.[54]

Gerhard Fricke's praise of Wackenroder as pioneer proved, if anything, even more emphatic:

In Wackenroder there sounded the earliest, the clearest, the most intimate and at the same time the simplest note of German romanticism. Brief as his life was, and scanty the work he left us, this life and this work is nevertheless the authentic beginning of romanticism. While his first piece, which appeared unsigned, could be attributed to Goethe and had manifold connections with the spirit of Herder, the few pages which the youth wrote more for himself than for any kind of a public already contained in embryo the entire later romantic poetry of nature, the forthcoming romantic experience of music, the rediscovery of medieval art by brothers Boisserée, the magic of Jean Paul, and the life *problematik* of the romantic novel.[55]

As to Wackenroder's influence, present-day scholarship is still increasing its scope and impact. To cite a single example, a recent study concerning V. F. Odoyevsky notes that

Odoyevsky's conception of artistic "biography" appears to be particularly close to that of Wilhelm Heinrich Wackenroder, with whom he shares a number of other romantic ideas (such as the inadequacy of language, the work of art as a hieroglyph and the religiously symbolic significance of art). Particularly striking is the mystical vision of religion and art which the young Sebastian undergoes in his nocturnal visit to the church in Eisenach; this is very similar to the religious experience of music at the rotunda in Wackenroder's "Letter of a Young German Painter in Rome to His Friend in Nuremberg."[56]

52. Wackenroder and Tieck, *Herzensergiessungen*, p. ix.
53. Ibid., p. xxxviii.
54. Ibid., p. xii.
55. Fricke, "Bemerkungen," p. 345.
56. Neil Cornwell, *The Life, Times, and Milieu of V. F. Odoyevsky, 1804–1869* (Athens, Ohio, 1986), p. 48.

But Wackenroder himself did not live to enjoy his reputation and influence. He died in 1798, at the age of twenty-four, as a result, we are usually told, of a nervous collapse (although the medical diagnosis of typhoid also exists) caused by the pressure of life and, more specifically, by a continuous confrontation with his father, an official who wanted his son to take up a useful and practical profession rather than devote himself to art and music.

III

Although Wackenroder—like Wordsworth and Novalis—was possessed by a vision, rather than by intellectual constructs, and although his work may well be described as "an independent growth," he did belong to the small group of literati in whose midst German romantic theory emerged. Gillies even asserted that "by creating while others theorized, Tieck and Wackenroder provided an immediate literary basis for their fellow-Romanticists to build upon."[57] Be this as it may (and it seems extremely likely that Wackenroder profited from, as well as contributed to, the efforts of his romantic associates), romantic theory became established in Germany at the very end of the eighteenth century, at the same time that Wordsworth and Coleridge introduced romanticism into English literature and thought. Friedrich Schlegel assumed the role of its foremost ideologist and prophet; and *Athenaeum,* the periodical which he published from 1798 to 1800, served as the main organ of the new dispensation. More exactly, in the words of two specialists:

> If one were to characterize the tasks with which the members of the school chiefly occupied themselves, one could say that Friedrich Schlegel was the theoretical thinker, the philosopher, his brother August Wilhelm Schlegel was the philologist and literary historian, and Friedrich Schleiermacher the moralist and theologian of the "Romantic Academy." Ludwig Tieck was the most successful popular storyteller and Novalis (Baron Friedrich von Hardenberg) may be regarded as the mystical and esoteric poet of the group.[58]

Friedrich Schlegel was born on March 10, 1772, in Hanover and died on January 12, 1829, in Dresden. A brilliantly gifted and precocious intellectual—"always provoking and always provoked and a veritable burning

---

57. Wackenroder and Tieck, *Herzensergiessungen,* p. xii.

58. Friedrich Schlegel, *Dialogue on Poetry and Literary Aphorisms,* ed. Ernst Behler and Roman Struc (University Park, Pa., 1968), p. 4. On *Athenaeum,* see, esp., Alfred Schlagdenhauffen, *Frédéric Schlegel et son groupe: La doctrine de l'Athenaeum, 1798–1800,* (Paris, 1934). I used the original edition of *Athenaeum* (Berlin) available at the Library of Congress (vols. 1–3 [1789–1800], as well as later republications and translations of articles from it, as cited in my footnotes. Helmut Schanze considered 1799 as the *Wendepunkt* in the establishment of German romanticism (*Romantik und Aufklärung: Untersuchungen zu Friedrich Schlegel und Novalis,* 2d enl. ed. [Nuremberg, 1976], p. 151).

brand," according to Goethe[59]—he had already traveled a long road before he became the ideologist of German romanticism. That road included education at the universities of Göttingen, Leipzig, and Dresden, and a general Enlightenment and classical orientation, together with a special concentration on the literatures of ancient Greece and Rome, which resulted in such studies as *On the Schools of Greek Poetry* (1794) and *A History of the Literature of the Greeks and Romans* (1798). Constantly engaged in intellectual search and speculation, Friedrich Schlegel hit his stride when he discovered in romanticism a field of his own to explore and exploit, and proceeded to do so on the pages of *Athenaeum* and elsewhere.

In the celebrated fragment 116 Friedrich Schlegel defined the crucial concept of romantic poetry:

> Romantic poetry is a progressive, universal poetry. Its aim isn't merely to reunite all the separate species of poetry and put poetry in touch with philosophy and rhetoric. It tries to and should mix and fuse poetry and prose, inspiration and criticism, the poetry of art and the poetry of nature; and make poetry lively and social, and life and society poetical; poeticize wit and fill and saturate the forms of art with every kind of good, solid matter for instruction, and animate them with the pulsations of humor. It embraces everything that is purely poetic, from the greatest systems of art, containing within themselves still further systems, to the sigh, the kiss that the poetizing child breathes forth in artless song. It can so lose itself in what it describes that one might believe it exists only to characterize poetical individuals of all sorts; and yet there is still no form so fit for expressing the entire spirit of an author; so that many artists who started out to write only a novel ended up by providing us with a portrait of themselves. It alone can become, like the epic, a mirror of the whole circumambient world, an image of the age. And it can also—more than any other form—hover at the midpoint between the portrayed and the portrayer, free of all real and ideal self-interest, on the wings of poetic reflection, and can raise that reflection again and again to a higher power, can multiply it in an endless succession of mirrors. It is capable of the highest and most variegated refinement, not only from within outwards, but also from without inwards; capable in that it organizes—for everything that seeks a wholeness in its effects—the parts along similar lines, so that it opens a perspective upon an infinitely increasing classicism. Romantic poetry is in the arts what wit is in philosophy, and what society and sociability, friendship and love are in life. Other kinds of poetry are finished and are now capable of being fully analyzed. The romantic kind of poetry is still in the state of becoming; that, in fact, is its real essence: that it should forever be becoming and never be perfected. It can be exhausted by no theory and only a divinatory criticism would dare try to characterize its ideal. It alone is infinite, just as it alone is free; and it recognizes as its first commandment that the will of the poet can tolerate no law above itself. The

---

59. Ernst Behler, *Friedrich Schlegel in Selbstzeugnissen und Bilddokumenten* (Hamburg, 1966), p. 46.

romantic kind of poetry is the only one that is more than a kind, that is, as it were, poetry itself: for in a sense all poetry is or should be romantic.[60]

Friedrich Schlegel's protean program for romantic poetry and poets could have been signed by his friend Novalis, and it bore major resemblances to the views held and developed at the same time by Coleridge and Wordsworth. The poet, the artist, occupied center stage. As Friedrich Schlegel explained in another fragment, "What men are among the other creatures of the earth, artists are among men."[61] Not surprisingly, they were linked to both God and nature: "God is everything that is purely original and sublime, consequently the individual himself taken to the highest power. But aren't nature and the world also individuals?"[62] "The Being of God is as evident as that of nature, for both are parts of humanity."[63] All original and eternal individuals lived in the Universal Spirit. Poetry and philosophy were different spheres, forms or component parts of religion. As in Novalis' vision, poets, artists, and priests were really one. Christianity was of a fundamental importance, but it needed to be continued and developed: "The revolutionary desire to realize the kingdom of God on earth is the elastic point of progressive civilization, and the beginning of modern history. Whatever has no relation to the kingdom of God is of strictly secondary importance in it."[64] Christianity was indeed "a fact. But only a fact in its beginning stages."[65] As Alfred Lussky remarked in regard to Friedrich Schlegel, "One must not forget, in the first place, that his father, brother, and uncle were German Lutheran pastors."[66]

But while that strong and rich Lutheran background no doubt remained of significance, other basic elements had entered in. Like most early romanticists, Friedrich Schlegel had gone through a period of enlightened rationalism; and when he turned again to religion, the new religion could not be safely confined within Christianity, let alone strict Lutheranism. As Walter Silz put it, Friedrich Schlegel "conceived of a synthesis of Goethe's and Fichte's thought as the basis for a new religion."[67] Most apposite perhaps was the expression *der Messias der Natur* (the Messiah of nature), found especially in Novalis' notes, because the beliefs of both Friedrich Schlegel and Novalis had at the time a powerful messianic thrust. Friedrich Schlegel declared his

60. Friedrich Schlegel, *Friedrich Schlegel's "Lucinde" and the Fragments*, trans. Peter Firchow (Minneapolis, Minn., 1971), pp. 175–76. For one clear but perhaps too simple explanation of how Friedrich Schlegel reached this definition, see Hans Eichner, "The Genesis of German Romanticism," *Queen's Quarterly* 72, no. 2 (Summer 1965): 213–31.

61. Schlegel, *Schlegel's "Lucinde,"* p. 245.

62. Ibid.

63. Friedrich Schlegel, *Friedrich Schlegel: Schriften und Fragmente: Ein Gesamtbild seines Geistes*, ed. Ernst Behler (Stuttgart, 1956), p. 161.

64. Schlegel, *Schlegel's "Lucinde,"* p. 192.

65. Ibid.

66. Alfred Edwin Lussky, *Tieck's Romantic Irony, with Special Emphasis upon the Influence of Cervantes, Sterne, and Goethe* (Chapel Hill, N.C., 1932), p. 253, n. 140.

67. Silz, *Early German Romanticism*, p. 55.

intention to establish a new faith or at least to sponsor its establishment—a John the Baptist if not the Messiah. He wrote to Novalis, "I believe I shall found a new religion or rather help to proclaim it."[68] His grandiose plan to create a new Bible pursued the same purpose: "The aim of my literary project is to write a new Bible and to follow in the footsteps of Mohammed and Luther."[69] Yet it was in a strange novel, *Lucinde,* published in 1799, that Friedrich Schlegel's search for a faith and at the same time determination to proclaim that faith attained their most elaborate form.

To present Peter Firchow's analysis of the novel:

> The master key to the mystery of *Lucinde* is the recognition that it is first and foremost a religious book. At the time Schlegel was writing this novel, he became convinced of the necessity of a new religion and of his fitness to be its prophet. This "religion" was, of course, not to be a rigidly structured one; that would have gone too much against the grain of his critical thinking, as well as his personality. It was to be, rather, more in the nature of a new mythology, a new morality, and a new philosophy. *Lucinde* represents the first installment (the "erster Teil," as the original title page has it) of his new vision; it is not so much a novel in the conventional, traditional sense as it is a fusing together of fictionalized philosophy, figurative morality, and allegorical religion.
>
> There are numerous and continual references in *Lucinde* to support the contention that this is a religious book; references to Julius as a priest, Lucinde as a priestess, to both being purified, to his being anointed, to her being, at least in a vision, beatified. Indeed, the "Apprenticeship for Manhood," the longest single block of the novel, is concerned with the delineation of an increasingly intense spiritual crisis from which Julius is finally saved by Lucinde and by what Lucinde represents. The question which this whole section of the novel faces and attempts to resolve is the question of what and why one should believe, and how, in consequence, one is to act.
>
> The religion of which Julius and Lucinde are priest and priestess is the religion of love. Though in the abstract this may seem rather trite, in practice it is not so. For from this religion there follow certain rules of behavior which attack not merely the usual conceptions of morality, but also the customary sentimentalities of love. There are two main dogmas in this religion—at least as it is fragmentarily presented here—which, in turn, form the two main themes of the novel: the love of man for man, or friendship; and the love of man for woman; or passionate love. Friendship, it is made amply clear in the course of the novel, is possible only among men, for in Schlegel's conception, women are wholly passionate and consequently incapable of Platonic disinterestedness. But if woman's passionate nature is her weakness, it is also her strength, for unquestionably the love of woman is more significant and important for Schlegel than the love of man. It is not by accident that the title of the novel is identical with the name of its female rather than its male protagonist; at the center of Schlegel's new religion

---

68. Forstman, *Romantik Triangle,* p. 22.

69. M. Preitz, ed., *Friedrich Schlegel und Novalis: Biographie einer Romantikerfreundschaft in ihren Briefen* (Darmstadt, 1957), p. 130. The letter was dated October 20, 1798.

stands, quite unmistakably, the feminine ideal. Lucinde—a name derived from the Latin *lux,* meaning light—is Julius's illumination. Ironically, however, her light is not the light of day; it is, instead, as we can see from the section entitled "Yearning and Peace," the light of night, the light of the pale moon and stars. Lucinde, like Diana, is a priestess of the night, and, like Diana's symbol, the moon, her illumination is indirect and by reflection, as the moon reflects the light of the sun. The moon and the woman are mirrors, are passive, and the man who loves a woman truly sees his own light and his own image reflected in her; he loves himself, Narcissus-like, in her. The love of woman leads consequently, to a fuller awareness of self.[70]

Though woman is for Julius (and Schlegel) the most obvious and most important symbol and manifestation of nature's principle of passivity, she is not the only one. The plant and the night also occupy places of considerable importance in Schlegel's symbology. The plant represents passivity and unconsciousness par excellence, since it instinctually obeys the mandates of nature and does not need to discover rules by which to develop itself. Nature has taken care of all that already. The plant grows, blossoms, and withers in harmony with the seasons and the course of nature; it does not rebel against dying because it cannot be conscious of rebellion. It exists for nothing but itself; it is its own achievement and purpose. Mankind, on the other hand—at least perverted, conventional mankind—rebels against nature and makes its own rules. Man attempts to live according to ideals and purposes outside himself and outside nature. He seeks to impose his own consciousness upon nature. According to Schlegel, this is man's perversion. Man must be dis-educated from such falseness, and brought back to an awareness that he can achieve perfection only in passivity, or, as Julius remarks, in a state of *"pure vegetating."* Man must live like a plant; he must be passive and purposeless.[71]

A further symbol of passivity in the novel is the night. Lucinde is called the "priestess of the night," and it is apparent that she holds her office because it is the night which—at least in relation to the day—is passive. The night is the time of rest, of dreams rather than thought, but also of love and passion. For true passivity, according to Schlegel, does not mean inactivity, boredom, or laziness; it means, rather a passivity in relation to nature, a passivity which in turn makes man really and naturally creative. The word passion, in German ("Leidenschaft," from "leiden," to suffer) as in English (from the Latin "pati," to suffer), is derived from the same concept, that of suffering, of passivity, of being done to rather than doing; but, again both in English and German, the word passion denotes an emotional force of great power. Stated differently, passion is something which cannot be consciously willed, but only triggered by nature; and once released, it possesses enormous energy.

70. Schlegel, *Schlegel's "Lucinde,"* pp. 23–24. Cf. Friedrich Schlegel's "Ideen zu Gedichten" (Thoughts for Poems) dating from the same period, such as "Each true love is sole and entirely without end, it can only ascend eternally. Love is also the source of all poetry" (*Literary Notebooks, 1797–1801,* ed. Hans Eichner [London, 1957], p. 153, no. 1500) and "Love is the art of egoism; only through love does one become an individual" (*Schlegel's "Lucinde,"* p. 157, no. 1549; both translations are my own).

71. Ibid., pp. 25–26; italics in original.

Consequently, the truly creative and energetic man is one who is passive and in accordance with nature; he does not obey the arbitrary rules of reason or man, but succumbs instead to divine inspiration. The true artist lets his work of art grow, naturally and for itself alone.[72]

It is this plant analogy, Firchow continues, "which explains a good deal of the curious and otherwise inexplicable form of *Lucinde.*"[73] The novel was shapeless only in the traditional sense; considered in its own terms, it revealed its form.[74] In relation to early romanticism, Friedrich Schlegel's remarkable emphasis on passivity as the true creative stance parallels a similar and even more remarkable emphasis in Wordsworth, while the German critic's concept of the night brings to mind not only Novalis but also Coleridge, notably "The Rime of the Ancient Mariner" as interpreted by Robert Penn Warren.[75]

To be sure, at one level the novel is a highly personal autobiographical account of Friedrich Schlegel in the guise of Julius and his relationship to his mistress (later, wife) Dorothea Veit, the Lucinde of the title. It is this level that has tended to surprise by its candidness and even to scandalize various readers:

We see Julius at the beginning moving into a mood of spiritual despair in which everything loses meaning for him; then we watch him move gradually out of this despair as a result of his encounters with and loves for various women. And we see him, finally, gain peace spiritually and physically in his love for Lucinde, a love which releases within him his latent creative energies. Julius has rejected the values of conventional society, those unnatural and destructive values, and accepted in their place the values of nature, which are creative and constructive, and which convey to him for the first time a sense of the organic wholeness of his being. In discovering his love for Lucinde, Julius has discovered, as Schlegel says at the end of the third-person narrative, "the most beautiful religion."[76]

72. Ibid., p. 27.
73. Ibid.
74. "[*Lucinde,*] just as every flower and fruit, has a shape, but not the same shape every other flower or fruit does" (Ibid., p. 28). Firchow proceeded with an interesting analysis of both the peculiarities and the inner cohesion of the novel (Ibid., pp. 28–38). Its basic structure, at least, turned out to be lucid enough: "In a very rough way, the structure of *Lucinde* works as follows. The first six parts of the novel provide us with a picture of what Julius is, the central part shows us how he came to be what he is, and the last six parts adumbrate the further directions of his growth. This ordering corresponds more or less to the way we would normally approach any object in nature; first we observe what it is; then we inquire how it came be what it is; and, lastly, we speculate upon what it will become. Seen from this point of view, the form of *Lucinde* is definitely natural and organic" (Ibid., p. 32).
75. Robert Penn Warren, "A Poem of Pure Imagination: An Experiment in Reading," in *The Rime of the Ancient Mariner,* by Samuel Taylor Coleridge, (New York, n.d.), esp. pp. 86–89, 134–35. Robert Penn Warren concentrates on the nature and function of moonlight in Coleridge's work.
76. Schlegel, *Schlegel's "Lucinde,"* p. 34.

In a sense, the religion is uncomplicated: "Its rituals, we now see, are few and simple. Essentially there appear to be two which are important: the first a purification/confession, the removal of all misunderstandings between the lovers; and the second a consummation, sexual intercourse—or, to use Julius's phrase, 'appeasing the offended gods'."[77] But (as Silz and others have emphasized) the larger implications were always present: "For the young Friedrich Schlegel, love has an allegorical significance; it is a symbol for infinite love, which hovers in the background. The lover of Lucinde never loses his metaphysical sense; he loves, one might say, *sub specie universi*."[78] Or, to state the case in Friedrich Schlegel's own words: "God is love, that is not saying much; but God is a universe of love and a novel of worlds, that is very significant. God is created through the world."[79]

IV

Lucinde in fact remained unfinished; moreover, even when completed, it was meant to be but a part of a grandiose project.

> *Lucinde,* we can reasonably surmise, was planned as one of the four gospels in Schlegel's new religion; each further gospel was to present another respect of his religion until, with the last, St. Friedrich's evangelical work would have been accomplished. It is the idea of a progressively more complete revelation which also accounts for the mixture of formal techniques in *Lucinde:* letters, allegories, puns, symbols, fantasies, visions, dialogues, autobiography, prose poetry, and—in the unpublished continuation—rhymed poems. This mixture of forms represents an attempt to reflect formally the profusion and confusion of nature, the wealth of different forms which inhabit the universe. *Lucinde,* in other words, represents an attempt to portray not only thematically but also formally a spiritual and intellectual growth and union. The intellectual and spiritual transformations are accompanied by formal ones. This structural and thematic pattern, of course, matches exactly the one proposed by Schlegel in his fragment 116 with its doctrine of a progressive and universal poetry. And, ironically, in its incompleteness, *Lucinde* matches another part of this doctrine as well: for since it is incomplete, *Lucinde* can never *be* a novel, but must forever be attempting to *become* one.[80]

Whatever the exact reason, *Lucinde* remained a fragment or, at the most, an unfinished novel. The great project of which it was to constitute an integral part joined other schemes, whether proposed by Wordsworth, Coleridge,

77. Ibid., p. 33.
78. Silz, *Early German Romanticism,* p. 171.
79. Schlegel, *Schriften und Fragmenten,* p. 171.
80. Schlegel, *Schlegel's "Lucinde,"* pp. 38–39; italics in original. As Otto Mann put it, *Lucinde* was both the summit and the turning point of Friedrich Schlegel the romanticist (*Der junge Friedrich Schlegel* [Berlin, 1932], p. 204).

Novalis, or again by Friedrich Schlegel for that matter, in the remarkable romantic graveyard of such projects.

Moreover, its author, before long, was abandoning romanticism. The conversion to Roman Catholicism is appropriately considered as a definitive divide in Friedrich Schlegel's orientation and life, but it took a long time. The "transitional years" lasted from 1802 to 1808; and although the closest and most insightful student of the subject, F. Imle, assures us that his hero was "inwardly Catholic" from 1804 ("schon seit 1804 innerlich katholisch") and became a catechumen in 1805,[81] Friedrich Schlegel did not obtain a full and permanent membership in the Catholic church until 1808.

Friedrich Schlegel's retreat from romanticism proved to be both similar to and different from that of Wordsworth; and it is equally fascinating to the observer. As Imle and other commentators have noted, the German critic's newly found and, for him, desperately important Catholicism had a distinctive character: "It suffers in the first place from a lack of Christological clarity in his thought, as a result of which there is time and again error in the relationship of the absolute and the finite—the necessary and the contingent—in the essence and operation of the Godhead; or, at the very least, the attributes of the human nature of Christ are misplaced [*verlegt werden*] into his divine nature."[82] Friedrich Schlegel stressed the loving presence of God and opposed the view that God was incomprehensible to man. Together with the presence of God, collectivity—togetherness—he came to believe, marked Catholicism in contrast to Protestant individualism. Friedrich Schlegel's cherished hope (*Lieblingstraum*) was the coming of the age of the Holy Spirit; his favorite book in the Bible, the Apocalypse. On the other hand, it has been repeatedly remarked that sin and punishment—evil itself—received little or no attention from him.[83] As to more specific views, perhaps the most idiosyncratic (and a troublesome one for Catholic authorities) was his concept of divine pardon by God's making past transgressions not to have happened.[84]

81. Fanny Imle, *Friedrich von Schlegels Entwicklung von Kant zum Katholizismus,* (Paderborn, 1927), pp. 20, 92–178.

82. Imle, *Schlegels Entwicklung,* pp. 223–24.

83. There were exceptions to this generally correct observation, especially as regards fear of God. Also, as early as his *Athenaeum* period Friedrich Schlegel did declare, "The really central insight of Christianity is sin" (*Schlegel's "Lucinde,"* p. 247). For an extremely critical view of Friedrich Schlegel and his conversion to Catholicism see Karl Müller, *Friedrich Schlegels Konversion im Zusammenhang seiner weltanschaulichen Entwicklung* (Giessen, 1928). For Müller, Friedrich Schlegel's romantic theorizing was an effort to legitimize his own inadequacies (p. 37), while romantic thought as a whole signified a rebirth of primitive nonlogical thought (p. 84). The main weakness of the famous critic's religious constructs was to take similarity for identity (esp. p. 49). Other, more penetrating but also sharply critical accounts include Alfred von Martin, "Romantische Konversionen," *Logos* 17 (1928): 141–64, esp. pp. 141–59, and (in particular) Benno von Wiese, *Friedrich Schlegel: Ein Beitrag zur Geschichte der romantischen Konversionen* (Berlin, 1927). Wiese comments with regard to the romanticist's aforementioned preference for the Holy Spirit, "Within Friedrich Schlegel's idealistic Catholicizing philosophy the Father and the Son play no part" (p. 108).

84. Imle, *Schlegels Entwicklung,* p. 173.

The overall evaluations of Friedrich Schlegel's conversion to Catholicism range all the way from the claim that he found in the Roman church truth as well as unity and freedom, which he had been so fervently and fruitlessly pursuing, to the claim that by becoming Catholic he did, in effect, finally commit suicide.[85]

In politics, even more obviously than in religion, Friedrich Schlegel and Wordsworth followed similar ideological paths once they had turned away from romanticism. Naturally, Wordsworth would not have endorsed Schlegel's notorious assertion that constitutionalism was an English disease which politicians in other countries caught as they caught fever.[86] But, mutatis mutandis, the two were moving in the same direction of political and social conservatism and reaction. Already in 1808 Friedrich Schlegel transferred to Vienna; and in March 1809 he obtained the position of secretary in the imperial court and state chancery. His services to the Hapsburgs, often as writer or editor, were many and varied; and they kept him involved in European politics. In 1809 Friedrich Schlegel was present at the battle of Aspern in the suite of Archduke Charles; in 1814 and 1815 he worked on the German constitution for the Congress of Vienna; and from 1815 to 1818 he occupied the position of secretary of the Bundestag in Frankfurt. In general, in the post-Napoleonic period, the onetime stormy petrel, innovator, and progressive became a valuable functionary of the Metternichian system.

Friedrich Schlegel also continued to lecture, write, and publish. The former devotee of Fichte and theoretician of the "Romantic–Classical, organic–mechanical contrast"[87] transferred this dichotomy to the world of Restoration politics, which he had joined. According to one extreme opinion:

> The entire work of Schlegel is but a German response to Maistre's philosophy: about the Greeks, about the Russians, about the Jesuits, about Leibnitz, a great Christian and almost Catholic philosopher, and about Spinoza, a representative of "scientific Protestantism" and of "the spirit of negation," the man from Savoy and the convert of Cologne are in accord. The central

85. That last statement refers to the presence and persistence of the motif of suicide in Friedrich Schlegel's and Novalis' thought and later in the development of romanticism in a number of countries—a fact noted by many specialists. Thomas McFarland, for example, wrote: "Compare Friedrich Schlegel's *Lucinde:* 'For a human being who is a human being, there is no death other than his own self-induced death, his suicide'. Still further, compare Novalis: 'The authentic philosophical act is suicide; this is the real beginning of all philosophy" (*Romanticism and the Forms of Ruin: Wordsworth, Coleridge, and Modalities of Fragmentation* (Princeton, N.J., 1981), p. 15 n. 8). Karl Müller emphasized a letter from Friedrich Schlegel to his brother in which he wrote that for three years the thought of suicide had been his constant companion (*Schlegels Konversion,* p. 16). Primary sources and commentators on them could be easily multiplied. Unforgettable, of course, is Novalis' rapturous poetry to death. Novalis, however, did not commit suicide any more than Friedrich Schlegel, unless death from tuberculosis can be so interpreted.

86. Imle, *Schlegels Entwicklung,* p. 252.

87. René Wellek emphasized the seminal nature of the use of this concept by the brothers Schlegel in *Confrontations: Studies in the Intellectual and Literary Relations Between Germany, England, and the United States during the Nineteenth Century* (Princeton, N.J., 1965), p. 9.

idea of *The Philosophy of History* is the one that dominated *Evenings*, and especially that of the Senator.[88]

A more balanced judgement would allow the later Friedrich Schlegel more originality, as well as at least scattered brilliance. Nor was his influence on European intellectual life by any means limited to his early romantic period.[89] Like Coleridge, Friedrich Schlegel accomplished much in his later years; it is only that these accomplishments of the two men of letters bore little resemblance to "Kubla Khan" or to *Athenaeum*. Appropriately, when in 1823 Friedrich Schlegel came to edit and publish his works, he omitted *Lucinde* altogether.

Wackenroder died in 1798 following a nervous collapse and, apparently, after being stricken by typhoid. Novalis died of tuberculosis in 1801. Friedrich Schlegel began to shift his position in 1802 or thereabouts. These events together highlighted the end of the entire first stage of German romanticism, the so-called *Frühromantik* (early romanticism). In a classification representative of the scholarship on the subject, Paul Kluckhohn distinguished three stages of German romanticism: *Frühromantik,* beginning with Wackenroder's *Herzensergiessungen* in 1797 and lasting until August Wilhelm Schlegel's lectures in Berlin in 1802–4; *Jüngere Romantik* (young romanticism) centered in Heidelberg and continuing until about 1815; and *Spätromantik* (late romanticism), prominent in Vienna and Swabia but also in Dresden, Berlin, and (with Hoffmann) Silesia and extending into the 1830s.[90] Another specialist, H. A. Korff, emphasized the great break between *Frühromantik* and the following stage, which he designated (with many others) as *Hochromantik* (high romanticism). He dated the break around 1806 and described it as a transition from a transcendental and religious orientation to one that was practical, political, and national.[91] Still another leading scholar, Ernst Behler, concentrating on Friedrich Schlegel, ended his *frühromantisch* period with the Jena lectures of 1801.[92] Numerous other examples could be adduced to indicate both that *Frühromantik* has become an established concept in German

88. Robert Triomphe, *Joseph de Maistre: Étude sur la vie et sur la doctrine d'un matérialiste mystique* (Geneva, 1968), p. 548.

89. One of my own first scholarly discoveries was that A. S. Khomiakov's so-called history had as its intellectual basis Friedrich Schlegel's *Philosophy of History,* delivered as lectures in Vienna in 1828 and published there in two volumes in 1829. See my *Russia and the West in the Teaching of the Slavophiles: A Study of Romantic Ideology* (Cambridge, Mass., 1952), pp. 215–18. There I wrote, "It seems highly probable that Khomiakov borrowed the main idea from Schlegel and then developed it with his characteristic ingenuity and diffusiveness" (p. 218).

90. Paul Kluckhohn, *Das Ideengut der deutschen Romantik* (Tübingen, 1953), pp. 8–9. Cf. his *Persönlichkeit und Gemeinschaft: Studien zur Staatsauffassung der deutschen Romantik* (Halle, 1925). In English, Eugene N. Anderson relied heavily on Kluckhohn, fully acknowledging his debt, in his "German Romanticism as an Ideology of Cultural Crisis," *Journal of the History of Ideas* 2, no. 3 (June 1941); 301–17.

91. Korff, *Geist,* vol. 4, p. 15.

92. Ernst Behler, "Der Wendepunkt Friedrich Schlegels: Ein Bericht über unveröffentliche Schriften F. Schlegels in Köln und Trier," in *Romantikforschung seit 1945,* ed. Klaus Peter (Königstein, 1980), esp. p. 71.

intellectual history and that it has been frequently contrasted with the subsequent development of romanticism in Germany.

Some more specific studies of German romanticism have been particularly interesting and even surprising in regard to periods. To cite only one or two examples, Marshall Brown in his search for "the shape of German romanticism" discovered "the substitution, after 1800, of the ellipse with two centers for the circle as the basic romantic curve."[93] Alfred Edwin Lussky, studying irony in Tieck and developing Walter Silz's insight, concluded that the original romantic irony, as represented by Friedrich Schlegel, emphasized complete objectivity in creative work. It was Tieck and later romanticists who made irony subjective, author deliberately interfering with artistic creativity. "To recapitulate: Romantic irony was for Friedrich Schlegel *that objectivity in a romantic work of literary art which nevertheless shows forth plainly the literary creator in all his artistic power, glory, wisdom, and love toward his creation*"[94] and also "The true irony . . . is the irony of love."[95] By contrast, Tieck aimed ironically to destroy the objectivity of his work in order to demonstrate his freedom as sovereign artist and the transcendence of the ideal over any accomplishment.[96]

In Germany, as in England, romanticism emerged strikingly—indeed as an explosion—to be followed by collapse and retreat and to be succeeded by new romanticists, related to the original figures but also distinct and different. What, in effect, took place?

93. Marshall Brown, *The Shape of German Romanticism* (Ithaca, N.Y., 1979), p. 21. On romanticism and the circle, see also Georges Poulet, *Les métamorphoses du cercle* (Paris, 1961). According to Poulet, in the romantic context "man is thus simultaneously both center and circle: center through the active principle of his thought, circle through its infinite content" (p. 147).

94. Lussky, *Tieck's Romantic Irony*, p. 81; italics in original.

95. Ibid., p. 85—a very late statement, but it is Lussky's contention that Friedrich Schlegel never changed his view of irony. Cf. Wiese, Friedrich Schlegel, pp. 30–33.

96. Lussky, *Tieck's Romantic Irony*, p. 159. See Ingrid Strohschneider-Kohrs, *Die romantische Ironie in Theorie und Gestaltung* (Tübingen, 1960). See also Dieter Arendt, *Der "poetische Nihilismus" in der Romantik: Studien zum Verhältnis von Dichtung und Wirklichkeit in der Frühromantik*, 2 vols. (Tübingen, 1972), esp. vol. 1, pp. 20–25.

3

Some Observations on the Emergence of Romanticism

We were the first that ever burst
Into the silent sea.

COLERIDGE

There is an enormous scholarly literature on the nature and definition of romanticism. Nor does it exhibit consensus. In fact, some specialists denied the legitimacy of the generic term *romanticism,* arguing that one could effectively examine only different romanticisms.[1] Others, while not proscribing in principle the search for a unifying concept, pointed pessimistically to literally dozens and dozens of definitions, often mutually incompatible and even directly contradictory. Under the circumstances, certain experts resorted to purely external and formal classifications, designating the writers and the artists of a particular time period as romanticists and whatever they produced as romanticism. Romanticism has been linked especially to the id in contrast to classicism (linked to the superego) and realism (linked to the "reality principle"). A French critic commented that romanticism should be felt but never defined. There was even a brilliant, if unconvincing, effort to claim that the essence of romanticism was protest—the only definition that could perhaps bring all the others together. Still, most students of the subject have continued to use the concept of romanticism in the more or less traditional way and at the same time to supply it with some substantive meaning. The meaning has ranged from complex schemes with many variables to a highly selective listing of what the authors considered to be the essential and intrinsic

---

1. See, e.g., Arthur O. Lovejoy, *Essays in the History of Ideas* (Baltimore, Md., 1948), pp. 228–53.

elements of romanticism. To cite one of the best relatively recent defenses (so to speak) of the validity and usefulness of the concept of romanticism for scholarship and general understanding, René Wellek wrote in 1963:

> If we examine the characteristics of the actual literature which called itself or was called "romantic" all over the continent, we find throughout Europe the same conceptions of poetry and of the workings and nature of poetic imagination, the same conception of nature and its relation to man; and basically the same poetic style, with a use of imagery, symbolism, and myth which is clearly distinct from that of eighteenth-century neoclassicism.
>
> In all of these studies, however diverse in method and emphasis, a convincing agreement has been reached: they all see the implication of imagination, symbol, myth, and organic nature, and see it as part of the great endeavour to overcome the split between subject and object, the self and the world, the conscious and the unconscious. This is the central creed of the great romantic poets in England, Germany and France. It is a closely coherent body of thought and feeling.
>
> One could even say (if we did not suspect the word so much) that progress has been made not only in defining the common features of romanticism but in bringing out what is its peculiarity or even its essence and nature: that attempt, apparently doomed to failure and abandoned by our time, to identify subject and object, to reconcile man and nature, consciousness and unconsciousness by poetry which is "the first and last of all knowledge."[2]

While in profound sympathy with Wellek's and others' attempts to present a comprehensive and logical exposition and elucidation of romanticism, I am particularly interested here in the issue of origin—in the dazzling vision that made Wordsworth, Coleridge, Novalis, Wackenroder, and Friedrich Schlegel look at the world in a new way, illustrated and briefly narrated in the first two chapters. Forstman declared:

> Novalis, and then Schlegel, caught sight of a vision that dissolves time, transporting the visionary to a plane above change and temporality. It was related to the Orphic myth, the ancient mysteries, Gnosticism, neo-Platonism, the medieval Cathari, and to the speculations of Giordano Bruno, Jakob Böhme, Friedrich Oettinger, and Hemsterhuis, to name only a few members of the family. There would be other progeny both contemporary with Novalis and Schlegel and in the ages to come. The vision is likely to sprout at any time or place and may give every appearance of spontaneous generation. Father and mother may not be in evidence, but the family resemblance will be clear. With one variation or another, each will set a version of what is, if the term is permissible, the perennial religion—a vision of reality as a cosmic process of separation from and return to the One. Salvation consists in the ultimate reunification with or of the One—a *redintegration*

---

2. René Wellek, "The Concept of Romanticism in Literary History," in *Concepts of Criticism*, ed. Stephen G. Nichols, Jr. (New Haven, 1963), pp. 160–62, 220. For the quote from Wordsworth, see p. 14. Compare Wellek's various articles published in *Comparative Literature* as early as 1949.

in unum. This reintegration, of course, cannot be accomplished under conditions of this world, time, space and matter. These conditions bring about separation and alienation; they lead to measurement, calculation, manipulation, misunderstanding, collision, mistreatment, and suffering. Thus only a dissolution of the conditions—that is, of this world—can bring about unification.[3]

Not only Novalis and Friedrich Schlegel but also Wackenroder, Wordsworth, and Coleridge also caught sight of this vision or at least some very similar visions. In impact they were not unlike the visions experienced by the original apostles of Christianity and other seminal religious groups. As to the nature of the vision, Forstman mentions a number of possible sources (more could be cited), but the best general designation for their message and meaning would be *pantheism* or, perhaps, *panentheism.*

Pantheism, which equates God with the world (the world is God, and God is the world) goes back to the thought of classical antiquity and to various Oriental religions and philosophies. It has had a complicated history in the European Middle Ages and in modern times. Panentheism, the doctrine that God includes the world as a part, though not the whole, of his being, may be reducible to pantheism (Coleridge, among others, came eventually to believe this fervently); but it also attempts to provide a sphere of existence and activity for God independent of the world. Hence, panentheists may be able to refer to God in a more traditional way without necessarily committing error or anachronism. German specialists have frequently preferred panentheism to pantheism as the designation of early romantic faith.[4] Scholars in the English language (possible because of the enormous stature of Wordsworth, who in his great creative phase seemed to need no God outside nature) usually find the romantic "strange seas of thought" to be pantheism.[5] There have been important exceptions, to be sure. I was impressed by Ernest Lee Tuveson's recent presentation of romanticism as a direct product of the hermetic teaching—one of the many elements of the bouillabaisse on which Forstman centered his attention but also distinct, specific, and certainly panentheistic.[6]

---

3. Jack Forstman, *Romantic Triangle: Schleiermacher and Early German Romanticism* (Missoula, Mont., 1977), p. 116. The vision was sudden. Schleiermacher wrote, "All is immediately true in religion, for except immediately how could anything arise?" (*On Religion: Speeches to Its Cultured Despisers,* trans. John Oman (New York, 1958), p. 54. On time and romanticism, see Manfred Frank's strikingly Heideggerian study, *Das Problem "Zeit" in der deutschen Romantik: Zeitbewusstsein und Bewusstsein von Zeitlichkeit in der frühromantischen Philosophie und in Tiecks Dichtung* (Munich, 1972).

4. See, e.g., Carl Schmitt, *Politische Romantik* (Munich 1925), p. 134, and (with special reference to Novalis) Paul Kluckhohn, *Das Ideengut der deutschen Romantik* (Tübingen, 1953), p. 139. See also Max Deutschbein, *Das Wesen des Romantischen* (Cöthen, 1921).

5. Newton P. Stallknecht, *Strange Seas of Thought: Studies in William Wordsworth's Philosophy of Man and Nature,* 2d ed. (Bloomington, Ind., 1958).

6. Ernest Lee Tuveson, *The Avatars of Thrice Great Hermes: An Approach to Romanticism* (Lewisburg, Pa., 1982). Tuveson's previous major contribution to the study of romanticism was *The Imagination as a Means of Grace: Locke and the Aesthetics of Romanticism* (Berkeley, 1960).

Pantheism (or panentheism) implied that nature was alive. It was, indeed, alive for Novalis, as the passages from *The Novices of Sais* and other works I have quoted show. H. W. Piper, Jonathan Wordsworth, and others traced this belief on the part of Wordsworth perhaps back to 1792 and certainly to 1794. It was found in the French radical and revolutionary milieu which the poet discovered when he crossed the Channel, as well as in such English sources as Priestley.[7] "The crucial point in the history of English Romanticism," writes Piper, "came when the concept of the 'active universe' met the developing theory of the Imagination,"[8] which focused on the interaction between mind and nature. In the words of Jonathan Wordsworth, "When in the spring of 1798 Wordsworth wrote, 'in all things / He saw one life, and felt that it was joy . . . To every natural form, rock, fruit, and flower, / Even the loose stones that cover the highway, / He gave a moral life . . .' a major change had taken place in his way of thinking."[9] It was this symbiosis of one life embraced by Coleridge and by Wordsworth that led to the emergence of English romanticism. Wordsworth made perhaps the most remarkable statement of his new faith in a fragment belonging to the summer of 1799:

> I seemed to learn
> That what we see of forms and images
> Which float along our minds, and what we feel
> Of active or recognizable thought,
> Prospectiveness, or intellect, or will,
> Not only is not worthy to be deemed
> Our being, to be prized as what we are,
> But is the very littleness of life.
>
> Such consciousness I deem but accidents,
> Relapses from the one interior life
> That lives in all things, sacred from the touch
> Of that false secondary power by which
> In weakness we create distinctions, then
> Believe that all our puny boundaries are things
> Which we perceive, and not which we have made—
> In which all beings live with God, themselves
> Are God, existing in one mighty whole,
> As undistinguishable as the cloudless east
> At noon is from the cloudless west, when all
> The hemisphere is one cerulean blue.[10]

7. Herbert W. Piper, *The Active Universe: Pantheism and the Concept of Imagination in the English Romantic Poets* (London, 1962). Jonathan Wordsworth, *The Music of Humanity: A Critical Study of Wordsworth's "Ruined Cottage"* (London, 1969).

8. Piper, *Active Universe*, p. 2.

9. J. Wordsworth, *Music of Humanity*, p. 188.

10. Lawrence Lipking, ed., *High Romantic Argument: Essays for M. H. Abrams* (Ithaca, 1981), p. 60.

Coleridge, who also started from the belief in the "active universe," wide-spread in radical (and in his case most notably Unitarian) circles, and became the main architect of the concepts of one life and poetic imagination in English romanticism, made the point in a less grand but an equally decisive manner, in a private letter: "Nature has her proper interest: and he will know what it is, who believes and feels, that every Thing has a Life of it's [sic] own, and that we are all *one Life*."[11]

However, important as intercommunion with nature was in much of romantic theory and creativity (witness, again, the selections from Novalis) pantheism or panentheism demanded still more. Taken to its logical—and psychological—conclusion, the doctrine of one life meant that only that all-embracing one life really existed, whereas everything else was merely its detail. Treating these details as distinct, separate, or individual constituted (to refer back to Wordsworth) the erecting, through the weakness of our perception, of false boundaries corresponding to nothing in the universe. True knowledge and true being were to be found instead in Wordsworth's spots of time or in Novalis' longed-for absorption into the night, love, and cosmos. It is this fundamental and deeply felt conviction that made boundaries generally so blurred in romantic literature. Romantic descriptions of nature are characteristically deficient in realism, in spite of occasional marvelous specificity. People (except for the author's own encompassing and expanding pantheistic ego) lack individuality and independence. Sophie represented perhaps the greatest experience in the poet's life, while Lucy may not have existed at all; but they are both symbols rather than human beings in the great writing devoted to them. The entire romantic setting tends to fade out in "wise passiveness," moonlight, and reabsorption into the universe.[12]

Streams, water, liquidity served admirably this blurring of boundaries, for water could dissolve or overflow everything. Novalis's amazing paean to liquification that I have quoted expressed a fundamental romantic vision of the world. Not only nature in the ordinary sense of the term but people, too, dissolved: "In the golden age we lived like these waves; in variegated clouds, those floating seas and springs of life on earth, the generations of mankind loved and procreated in never-ending games."[13] Or, to repeat Wordsworth

No fountain from its rocky cave
E'er tripped with foot so free;

---

11. Herbert Lindenberger, *On Wordsworth's "Prelude"* (Princeton, 1963), p. 90; italics in original. The letter was written in 1802 to William Sotheby. As to Coleridge's artistic expression of this teaching, special attention is usually paid to "The Rime of the Ancient Mariner." For example, "The psychological unity of *The Ancient Mariner* lies in its full realization of the vital experience which the doctrine of the living universe offered the poet" (Piper, *Active Universe*, p. 105).

12. For a brilliant analysis of this romantic fade-out in the case of Lamartine's poetry, see Georges Poulet, *Les métamorphoses du cercle* (Paris, 1961), pp. 177–202.

13. Novalis, *The Novices of Sais,* trans. Ralph Manheim (New York, 1949), p. 105.

> She seemed as happy as a wave
> That dances on the sea.[14]

Wind, for its part, roamed even more freely than water; and it, too, swept through romantic literature.

In romanticism the so-called objective reality could fade out, dissolve in water, or fly away with the breeze. Perhaps even more remarkably, it could suddenly become something else—the boundaries and the identities were in flux. As in the case of the teacher of the novices of Sais:

> Soon he became attentive to the connections that are everywhere, to meetings and encounters. It was not long before he ceased to see anything by itself.—The perceptions of his senses crowded into great colorful images; he heard, saw, touched and thought at once. He delighted in bringing strangers together. Sometimes the stars were men for him and sometime men were stars, sometimes the stones were beasts, the clouds plants; he played with forces and phenomens; he knew where and how he could find this and that, or make this and that manifest itself; he himself plucked the strings in search of chords and melodies.[15]

As Novalis put it in his notes for *Heinrich von Ofterdingen,* Heinrich "becomes a flower—an animal—a stone—a star."[16] The reference to "chords and melodies" is very much to the point, because it was precisely in listening to music, his consuming passion, that Wackenroder felt boundaries dissolve and himself acquiring different identities. Music, unrestricted by physical form, place, and (in a sense) time became the ideal art of German romanticism and other romanticisms.

Until the repression and retreat, pantheism permeated Wordsworth's life, as well a his art. Newton P. Stallknecht quotes Wordsworth telling Coleridge, "In your religious talk with children say as little as possible about *making*" and referring to a four-and-a-half-year-old's seeing a bit of God in

14. William Wordsworth, *Poems,* ed. John O. Hayden, (Harmondsworth, Eng., 1977), vol. 1, p. 383. Compare, for instance, Irving Babbitt's observation: "The peasant is more poetical than the aristocrat because he is closer to nature, for Wordsworth as he himself avows, is less interested in the peasant for his own sake than because he sees in him a sort of emanation of the landscape.—Shepherds, dwellers in the valleys, men / Whom I already loved;—not verily / For their own sakes, but for the fields and hills / Where was their occupation and abode" (*Rousseau and Romanticism* [Boston, 1919], p. 145 and n. 1). As to the ultimate meaning of water for Wordsworth, consider, for instance, David Ferry's view: "The relation of man to eternity is not that of the perceiver of order to the order he perceives. It is that of the victim to the sea which will obliterate him. The waters of the deep are always gathering upon us" (*The Limits of Mortality: An Essay on Wordsworth's Major Poems* [Middletown, Conn., 1959], pp. 158–59). Geoffrey H. Hartmann emphasized near the end of his more optimistic analysis, *"In the imagination of Wordsworth everything tends to the image and sound of universal water."* (*The Unmediated Vision: An Interpretation of Wordsworth, Hopkins, Rilke, and Valéry* [New York, 1966], p. 43; italics in original).

15. Novalis, *Novices of Sais,* p. 9.

16. Novalis, *Novalis,* ed. Richard Samuel and Hans-Joachim Mähl (Munich, 1978), vol. 1, p. 392.

the rustle of the wind.[17] Death, like creation, had no place in the timeless and indivisible pantheistic universe. Wordsworth declared, "Nothing was more difficult for me in childhood than to admit the notion of death as a state applicable to my own being."[18] I conclude with some of the most famous examples of Wordsworthian pantheism, as presented by Bateson:

> How extreme that subjectivism had been can be seen from a passage in Wordsworth's note on "Intimations of Immortality." "I was often unable," he says, "to think of external things as having external existence, and I communed with all that I saw as something not apart from, but inherent in, my own immaterial nature. Many times while going to school have I grasped at a wall or tree to recall myself from the abyss of idealism to reality. . . ."
>
> Towards the end of his life, he told Bonamy Price, the Oxford economist, that there had been a time when he had to push against something that resisted to be sure there was anything outside himself. When making these avowals to Price, he suited the action to the word by clenching the top of a five-barred gate that they happened to be passing, and pushing against it with all his strength.[19]

To survive pantheism or panentheism, Friedrich Schlegel and Coleridge also grasped a wall, a tree, or a five-barred gate. Wackenroder and Novalis perished before they could grasp anything.

Wordsworth, as we know, proceeded to revise and expurgate his writings, the process that can be best observed in the repeated changes which he made in *The Prelude*. Artistically, these emendations were, both in general and in most specific cases, for the worse. Changes pointed in several directions. Wordsworth was becoming less radical, more patriotic—more English as against French, if you will. But, most important, he was eliminating—or at least attenuating and diminishing—his pantheism or panentheism. As the editors of the 1979 edition of *The Prelude 1799, 1805, 1850* expressed it, Wordsworth had "most conspicuously . . . toned down, by touches of Christian piety, the poem's more radical statements of the divine sufficiency of the human mind in its interchange with Nature."[20] There were several dozen such modifications, ranging from the obvious insertions of God where he had not been present earlier to replacing "As my soul bade me" with "As

17. Stallknecht, *Strange Seas,* p. 175; italics in original. See also Mary Moorman, *William Wordsworth: A Biography,* (Oxford, 1957, 1965), vol. 1, pp. 584–85.

18. Wordsworth, *Poems,* vol. 1, p. 978. There is no necessary contradiction between this dismissal of death and the longing for death on the part of Novalis and other romanticists. Wordsworth referred here to the conventional view of death. Novalis thought of death as an accentuation and affirmation of the eternal pantheistic unity. In the words of Coleridge: "Life seems to me then a universal spirit, that neither has nor can have an opposite. God is everywhere, I have exclaimed, and works everywhere; and where is there *room* for Death?" (*Collected Letters of Samuel Taylor Coleridge,* ed. Earl Leslie Griggs [Oxford, 1950–71], vol. 1, p. 916; italics in original).

19. F. W. Bateson, *Wordsworth: A Re-interpretation* (New York, 1956), p. 60.

20. William Wordsworth, *"The Prelude" 1799, 1805, 1850,* ed. Jonathan Wordsworth, M. H. Abrams, and Stephen Gill (London, 1979), p. xii.

piety ordained"[21] and *he* with *it* as the pronoun for a breeze.[22] Capitalization of common nouns drastically declined. Remarkably, at the end of this process of change, *The Prelude* could still be read, at least in large part, as a pantheistic document—a tribute to the power of Wordsworth's original vision. Indeed, Selincourt had some reason to write of Wordsworth's "disguising his former faith."[23] More fairly, the evolution of *The Prelude* represented both a genuine attempt to escape from persistent pantheism and a hectic effort to cover its tracks—both endeavors operating, apparently, at several levels of consciousness. Wordsworth not only assumed the orthodox religious position, as professed by the Anglican Church, but also became a proponent of political and social conservatism—even reaction—and a leading man of letters of the British establishment. He also stopped writing great poetry.

Friedrich Schlegel grasped at Roman Catholicism. The transition from pantheism or panentheism to Catholicism was a difficult one, and it lasted some six years, from 1802 to 1808.[24] The end result gave the German critic, it would seem, some confidence and stability, as well as a determination to champion his new views. Like Wordsworth, Friedrich Schlegel combined religious orthodoxy with political conservatism. Eventually he became a prominent figure in the Metternichian, if not the Victorian, establishment. As with Wordsworth, the pantheist vision continued to trouble him. I noted earlier, following Imle, how Friedrich Schlegel's fervent Catholicism emphasized the immediate presence of God; the divine rather than the human nature of Christ; the coming age of the Holy Spirit; the Apocalypse; and even a doctrine of divine pardon whereby making past transgressions never to have

21. Ibid., pp. 428–29.

22. Ibid., p. 29.

23. Ibid., p. 524. Inevitably, the poet's treatment of nature became a central issue and difficulty of the literary criticism dealing with Wordsworth. For a single perceptive and complex example, see Thomas M. Raysor, "The Themes of Immortality and Natural Piety in Wordsworth's Immortality Ode," *Publications of the Modern Language Association of America* 69 (Sept.–Dec. 1954): 861–75. Raysor concluded: "In both the Ode and the *Excursion,* the mind sinks through pain to a level of thought deeper than pain; but in 1845, when the passage quoted from the *Excursion* appears first in print, the deeper level is that of Christian faith and hope. In the Ode it might possibly be the same, since it is after all the Immortality Ode. But I hesitate to argue the point, as I have before, for in this context of the last stanza, nothing more is directly suggested than the softening of the heart to sympathy by the love both of nature and of man. And even in the *Excursion,* the Christian consolation is a late addition. In the 1798 MS. version of this part of the *Excursion* and even in the printed text until 1845 Wordsworth sought for consolation in nature, but only in the impersonal, impassive beauty which makes one forget personal grief and even individual personality" (ibid., p. 875).

24. See, esp., F. Imle, *Friedrich von Schlegels Entwicklung von Kant zum Katholizismus* (Paderborn, 1927), pp. 92–178. See also Heinrich Newe, "Die Philosophie Friedrich Schlegels in den Jahren 1804–06," *Philosophisches Jahrbuch der Görresgesellschaft,* 43, no. 3 (1930): 272–87. Of Friedrich Schlegel's own writings, see esp. *Philosophische Vorlesungen (1800–1987),* vol. 1, ed. Jean-Jacques Austett, Kritische Friedrich Schlegel Ausgabe, vol. 12 (Munich, 1964), pp. 130–35. See also his *Über die Sprache und Weisheit der Indier,* ed. Ernst Behler and Ursula Struc-Oppenberg, Kritische Friedrich Schlegel Ausgabe, vol. 8 (Munich, 1975), pp. 242–53.

occurred. In a sense, time, space, identity, and discrete events remained unreal for Friedrich Schlegel.

The case of Coleridge was complex. The most common interpretation presents the poet as a Unitarian (Coleridge had become a Unitarian at Cambridge in 1793) proponent of the pantheistic or panentheistic doctrine of one life, which he managed to impose on his new friend, William Wordsworth, to produce English romanticism. Wordsworth, for his part, was no ideologist; but he was prepared by his own psychological and poetic experience (notably by the spots of time and in general by his pantheistic vision of the world) to receive Coleridge's theory. While this simplistic account may contain much truth, it would be misleading to assign a purely passive intellectual role to Wordsworth and even more misleading to forget Coleridge's own vision. After all, "The Rime of the Ancient Mariner" and "Kubla Khan" are among the greatest visionary poems in all literature. The relationship between the two authors of *Lyrical Ballads* was intricate, symbiotic, even uncanny. The eventual mutual decision that Coleridge would become the philosopher, and Wordsworth the poet, of the new dispensation deserves attention for more than one reason. While its positive content—that is, what the two intended to accomplish—received almost undivided attention, the decision constituted also a remarkable self-denying ordinance (or, rather, ordinances). Not only was Wordsworth to continue writing poems in his usual, rather isolated way, without having to theorize about them (that is, without first trying to bring them fully to his consciousness), but Coleridge, the other great poet, in effect, renounced writing poetry.

What motivated Coleridge during his symbiotic relationship with Wordsworth and after? McFarland makes a good case for the central role of pantheism (especially Spinoza's) and Coleridge's developing lifelong struggle against that teaching and that man. The relationship was typically one of love–hate and of the inability to break loose.

> Coleridge walked with me to A. Robinson's for my Spinoza, which I lent him. While standing in the room he kissed Spinoza's face in the title-page, and said, "This book is a gospel to me." But in less than a minute he added, "his philosophy is nevertheless false. Spinoza's system has been demonstrated to be false, but only by that philosophy which has demonstrated the falsehood of all other philosophies. Did philosophy commence with an *it is,* instead of an *I am,* Spinoza would be altogether true." And without allowing a breathing time, Coleridge parenthetically asserted, "I, however, believe in all the doctrines of Christianity, even the Trinity."[25]

25. Thomas McFarland, *Coleridge and the Pantheist Tradition* (Oxford, 1969), p. 254. Crabb Robinson's *Diary* refers precisely to October 3, 1812, but McFarland believes that this occurrence was illustrative of Coleridge's long-term relationship to Spinoza. Compare Coleridge's statement: "Not one man in a thousand has either strength of mind or goodness of heart to be an atheist. I repeat it. Not one man in ten thousand has goodness of heart or strength of mind to be an atheist. And, were I not a Christian . . . I should be an atheist with Spinoza. . . . This, it is

McFarland argued that the specific quality—in fact the greatness and the relevance—of Coleridge as a modern intellectual was precisely his refusal (inability, I should say) to confine himself to either horn of the dilemma: the "gray"—to use Goethe's pregnant terminology—realm of "correct" doctrine or the "green" world of ebullient pantheistic life:

> Thus Coleridge could complete no *opus maximum*. He could produce no system. He has been scorned by the uncomprehending and the academically inert. But his mind played between its two poles with matchless vitality.[26]

> In this equipoise Coleridge's philosophical achievement is both of its time and out of its time. His thought shares with that of his German contemporaries an emphasis upon the central importance of Spinozistic pantheism. But it differs in its idiosyncratic refusal to decide, either by pantheism or by solipsistic skepticism, that which cannot be decided.[27]

I would suggest, however, that whatever the larger problems connected with *opus maximum,* Coleridge's immediate motivation to discontinue the writing of great poetry was to escape danger.

Every reader of Coleridge knows that his poetic world was green and ebullient; and it tended to be pantheistic or panentheistic. To quote a few lines that impressed McFarland:

> So will I build my altar in the fields,
> And the blue sky my fretted dome shall be,
> And the sweet fragrance that the wild flower yields
>   Shall be the incense I will yield to Thee,
> Thee only God![28]

Yet Coleridge's thought—as distinct from his artistic creativity—came to be directed relentlessly against pantheism: "Now the very purpose of my system is to overthrow Pantheism, to establish the diversity of the Creator from the sum whole of his Creatures, deduce the personeity, the I Am of God, and in one and the same demonstration to demonstrate the reality and originancy of Moral Evil, and to account for the fact of a finite Nature."[29] Christianity— the concept of the Holy Trinity, which resolved the otherwise irresolvable dilemma of the choice between the one and the many—constituted the only

---

true, is negative atheism; and this is, next to Christianity, the purest spirit of humanity!" (Ibid., p. 251; ellipses McFarland's). "Even the Trinity" became Coleridge's anchor of salvation. Twenty-two years later, J. W. Green, who was present at the poet's deathbed, reported that his final words had been to repeat "his formula on the Trinity" (Stephen M. Weissman, M.D., *His Brother's Keeper: A Psychobiography of Samuel Taylor Coleridge* [Madison, Conn., 1989], p. 324).

26. McFarland, *Coleridge and the Pantheist Tradition,* p. 110.
27. Ibid., p. 254.
28. Ibid., p. 253. The poem "To Nature" has been dated as late as 1815 and even 1820.
29. McFarland, *Coleridge and the Pantheist Tradition,* p. 252.

valid and impregnable foundation for religion and morality. The pantheistic belief that everything was God, meant in fact that pantheism recognized no God and was, thus, a form of atheism. Panentheism, Unitarianism, and other sectarian creeds which stopped short of the Trinitarian dogma had no firm basis and were unavoidably reducible to pantheism. Spinoza's system might have been the right preference in a universe without Christ and the Holy Trinity, but it melted in the light of divine truth.

Other critics also noted the dichotomy and ambivalence in Coleridge so trenchantly presented and analyzed by McFarland. James D. Boulger commented that "Coleridge's earlier poems, preceding 1802, were in structure and ideas informed by the doctrines of immanence and pantheism; they reflected the breakdown in modern thought of the old beliefs about the composition of body and soul, and the collapse of the dichotomous scholastic logic which influenced earlier English poets."[30] These poems were successful, whereas "given . . . the emotional failure in the late poetry, it is no surprise that Coleridge is not remembered as a great Christian poet."[31] J. B. Beer even wrote of the later Coleridge: "It is the picture of a man who seeks to devote himself completely to the realization of a single vision, and who yet finds that that vision must be largely hidden from the world."[32] T. S. Eliot simply stated, "For a few years he had been visited by the Muse . . . and thenceforth was a haunted man."[33]

II

When its inherent tensions are considered, it may be more remarkable that early romanticism existed at all than that it lasted only a few years. Moreover, it exercised a strong influence on later romanticisms and even on the entire intellectual and artistic development of the Western world. However, before turning to even a very brief commentary on the fortunes of romanticism, it is appropriate to focus on one main element of the romantic equation—God.[34]

The supreme claim of pantheism or panentheism was to make men and women God. More precisely, they were parts of God; but because all divisions were ultimately unreal, they were, in effect, God himself (herself may be equally suitable here). As Tuveson emphasized in the case of his favorite panentheism—hermeticism—"We can draw one of the most audacious conclusions of all. To understand God, we must *become* gods. 'If then you do not

30. James D. Boulger, *Coleridge as Religious Thinker* (New Haven, 1961), p. 197.

31. Ibid., p. 199.

32. John B. Beer, *Coleridge the Visionary* (London, 1959), p. 41.

33. Ibid., p. 43.

34. Of the huge literature on romanticism and religion, I would mention first: M. H. Abrams, *Natural Supernaturalism: Tradition and Revolution in Romantic Literature* (New York, 1971). My Oxford teacher, Hans G. Schenk, subjected romanticism to a penetrating criticism from a narrowly Roman Catholic point of view in *The Mind of the European Romantics: An Essay in Cultural History* (London, 1966). As an example of a vast body of literature interpreting romanticism as a search for God, see, e.g., Fritz Strich, *Deutsche Klassik und Romantik oder Vollendung und Unendlichkeit, ein Vergleich* 3d ed. (Munich, 1928).

make yourself equal to God, you cannot apprehend God; for like is known by like'."[35] This corresponds admirably to the famous lines by Novalis, which I previously quoted:

> Kurz um, ich sah, dass jetzt auf Erden
> Die Menschen sollten Götter werden.
>
> And shortly, I saw, that now on earth
> Men must become Gods.[36]

As Wordsworth has it:

> . . . All beings live with God, themselves
> Are God, existing in one mighty whole,
> As undistinguishable as the cloudless east
> At noon is from the cloudless west, when all
> The hemisphere is one cerulean blue.[37]

Friedrich Schlegel wanted a new Bible and a new religion, which he could perhaps serve as a Mohammed or a Luther. *Lucinde* was part of a project to create such a religion. Who, then, creates religions? Novalis, who was linked closely to Friedrich Schlegel in the emergence of romanticism in Germany, left behind him such tantalizing concepts as the already-cited Messiah of nature. His most succinct formulation of the matter was stark indeed: "Gott ist Ich" ("God is I").[38]

We should consider this entire line of thought and belief very seriously. The spots of time and the longing to be absorbed into the night, death, nature, and love were the deepest experiences of Wordsworth and Novalis, respectively. *Magischer Idealismus* (magical idealism) was true and real for its adepts—literal, not figurative, allegorical, or symbolic. (Any present-day association of *magical* with make-believe or fakery is here extremely unfortunate.) A colleague argued ably with me that nevertheless, modern European intellectuals could not seriously believe that they were God or start a major intellectual movement on that basis. My suspicion is that they could and did.

Of course, the early romantic vision and synthesis did not endure. In fact,

---

35. Tuveson, *Avatars,* p. 28; italics in original.

36. Novalis, *Novalis,* vol. 1, p. 140. Compare Friedrich Schlegel's fragment no. 262 in *Athenaeum:* "Every good human being is always progressively becoming God. To become God, to be human, to cultivate oneself are all expressions that mean the same thing" (Schlegel, *Friedrich Schlegel's "Lucinde" and the Fragments,* trans. Peter Firchow [Minneapolis, Minn., 1971], p. 220).

37. Lipking, *High Romantic Argument,* p. 60.

38. Friedrich Hiebel, *Novalis: deutscher Dichter, europäischer Denker, christlicher Seher,* 2d ed. (Bern, 1972), p. 135. Hiebel provided some context for the statement. And it was Novalis whom Friedrich Schlegel addressed with "You are, without any doubt, destined to be the new Messiah; you will find in me a fervent apostle" (Novalis et al., *Novalis Schriften,* ed. Paul Kluckhohn and Richard Samuel [Leipzig, 1929], volume 4, p. 248).

one of the very few points of agreement about romanticism in general has been its volatility, fragmentariness, and frequently catastrophic character. To quote a brief, but typical, assessment by Virgil Nemoianu:

> This core of the romantic model and purest form—the possible–impossible expansion of the self to a seamless identification with the universe—is unstable and explosive. . . . The paradisiacal recovery of unity, the obliteration of analytical division, cannot be maintained long in purity, not even as an impression or as an aim. The brew does not age well, not because it is too weak, but because it is too strong. The almost mystical intensity of core romanticism cannot survive long. The model is too ambitiously designed. This explains why early death becomes almost a norm. Core romanticism results in suicide, misadventure, disease, drugs, madness, and the guillotine as exemplified by Kleist and Shelley, Byron and Novalis, Keats and Hölderlin, and Saint-Just—or alternatively deterioration and silence.[39]

Whereas the early romantic vision and synthesis vanished, their various elements reappeared in different combinations in subsequent romantic teachings and artistic practice. To follow this process, we should try to establish what became central in numerous romantic ideologies and also to keep in mind the relationship of romantics to their beliefs.

As to the issue of centrality, it may well be maintained that disagreement and pluralism existed among the romanticists from the start of the movement and that they could be overcome only briefly and with a strenuous effort by the all-absorbing pantheistic vision. Marshall Brown illustrated the situation tellingly from the notebooks of Friedrich Schlegel, one of the most restless romanticists: " 'Poetry is thoroughly central in every respect'; 'religion is the central center, that is clear'; 'only nature is central'; mythology or love is the center of poetry; reason is in the center; the golden age or the encyclopedia is the central center; music is center and periphery; 'yoni[40] is the present, center fullness'."[41] Following the collapse of early romanticism, such elements of its vision as nature, love, beauty, music, art, and artistic creativity developed more independently, separately, or in combination with other elements, inspiring their own theories and cults, while the argument about centrality continued for decades.

39. Virgil Nemoianu, *The Taming of Romanticism: European Literature and the Age of Biedermeier* (Cambridge, Mass., 1984), p. 27. For one of the most striking longer summaries of this kind, see Thomas McFarland, *Romanticism and the Forms of Ruin: Wordsworth, Coleridge, and Modalities of Fragmentation* (Princeton, 1981), pp. 15–20.

40. *Webster's New International Dictionary*, 2d ed., s.v. "yoni" says, "*Hindu Myth.* A figure representing the female genitals, serving as the formal symbol under which shakti, or the personification of the female power in nature, is worshipped."

41. Marshall Brown, *The Shape of German Romanticism* (Ithaca, 1979), p. 15, n. 2. The importance of the concept of the *center* (derived from Boehme) for Friedrich Schlegel is richly—indeed exaggeratedly—presented in Marie Joachim, *Die Weltanschauung der Romantik* (Jena, 1905). Compare Otto Mann's study of Friedrich Schlegel with its emphasis on Schlegel's frantically seeking solution, or rather salvation (*die Erlösung*) in one direction after another (*Der junge Friedrich Schlegel: Eine Analyse von Existenz und Werk* [Berlin, 1932]).

If the content of their beliefs frequently divided romanticists, their attitude toward their ideals was usually remarkably similar. The contrast between the finite and the infinite, frantic and heroic striving yet inability to attain the goal, enormous reach and inadequate grasp dominated the romantic scene. The greatest poets and writers of Europe claimed in despair that they could not adequately express themselves, a problem that had never occurred, for instance, to Voltaire. Vast projects, as we know, remained unwritten or at least unfinished. Longing and ecstasy combined with a crushing sense of inadequacy and unworthiness.

There is only one convincing explanation for this remarkable romantic paradox: a transfer of fundamental and traditional Christian beliefs and attitudes into the new romantic setting. That the romanticists were trying to reach God has been perceived by many critics. M. H. Abrams and some other scholars have also discovered how very deeply romanticism was rooted, in general, in Christian culture. Perhaps more emphasis might be placed on the quasi identity of the central romantic paradox and the basic Christian orientation: the finite and the infinite, continuous struggle unto death toward the ideal, man and God (except that the essence of God was changing). Human inability adequately to address God, speak of God, or praise God is, of course, a commonplace in Christianity. Paul Tillich observed that romanticism in philosophy consisted of the thesis that the infinite is present in the finite and the finite is able to penetrate the infinite. The qualities of and attitudes toward the Christian God devolved upon his romantic modifications and surrogates. To be sure, the view of human life as incessant striving toward an unattainable ideal is not limited to Christian thought. Other teachings which affirm it and are relevant for our purposes include Platonism and German idealistic philosophy (especially as presented by Kant and developed by Fichte). Fichte, in particular, has repeatedly been cited as the intellectual father of romanticism. But it seems best, at least in very general overall terms, to treat Kant and Fichte, and also Platonism in its various forms in 1750 or 1800 in Europe, as part of the Christian amalgam and worldview, which had dominated European perception for many centuries.[42]

The compelling power of romanticism serves to underline the point. Modern readers are frequently bored, annoyed, or even disgusted by the endless replaying of the *mal du siècle,* of the romantic agony, whether on the subject of love, friendship, artistic creativity, or other pursuits and by what the psychologists would call the persistent nonadjustive response of the protagonists. Although everything indicates the need to abandon a particular line of behavior and try something else, the romanticists (even when they themselves see this) nevertheless continue on their old hopeless course. But then,

---

42. The connection between German idealistic philosophy and its Christian background has not yet been sufficiently appreciated. A recent book redressed the balance in one important instance, Laurence Dickey's *Hegel: Religion, Economics, and the Politics of Spirit, 1770–1807* (New York, 1987). Another recent study emphasized tellingly some important Protestant elements in the German cultural evolution in the eighteenth century, Anthony J. La Vopa's *Grace, Talent, and Merit: Poor Students, Clerical Careers, and Professional Ideology in Eighteenth-Century Germany* (New York, 1988).

by definition, one cannot escape God. It is this religious subtext that might give profound meaning even to such an artistically brilliant but psychologically and humanly miserable document as Alfred de Musset's *Confession d'un enfant du siècle.*

Apparently (many colleagues tell me), romanticism was produced only by Western Christian civilization. It appeared nowhere else—except, of course, as translated and otherwise adapted from Europe. In my view, it would be likely to emerge independently only if another civilization had a concept of God and of man's relation to God at least very similar to the Christian.

To repeat, after the original romantic vision exploded or faded out, its elements reappeared in different combinations in subsequent romanticisms. The persistent romantic emphasis on nature is perhaps the most obvious example of this continuity. As C. M. Bowra put it, linking the early and the later romanticists and exaggerating the point: "In nature all the Romantic poets found their initial inspiration. It was not everything to them, but they would have been nothing without it; for through it they found those exalting moments when they passed from sight to vision and pierced, as they thought, to the secrets of the universe."[43] Not only poets predisposed to belief in a living universe and pantheism, such as Shelley, but even those quite differently inclined paid at least occasional tribute to the new mode. It was Byron who wrote the striking lines

> My altars are the mountains and the Ocean,
> Earth—air—stars,—all that springs from the great Whole,
> Who has produced, and will receive the Soul.[44]

Recently Sarah Pratt, writing on Russian romanticism, distinguished five concepts of nature among the poets and writers of that eclectic and somewhat confusing period: (1) a static setting for human activity, (2) the impetus for poetic reverie, (3) a mirror of the human soul, (4) man's partner in the metaphysical universe, and (5) the Absolute, "the source, the point of return, and the measure of all phenomena of the universe including man."[45] Except for the first (the older, classical view) all are relevant to the romantic perspective I have been trying to suggest. Beyond literature, the romantic cult of nature affected the arts, in the first place, painting—a subject outside my very brief commentary.[46]

Whereas the romantic preoccupation with nature spread very widely, it

43. C. M. Bowra, *The Romantic Imagination* (New York, 1961), p. 13.

44. Ibid., p. 160. For other similar passages in Byron, see: M. H. Abrams, *The Mirror and the Lamp: Romantic Theory and Critical Tradition* (New York, 1953), p. 347, n. 77.

45. Sarah Pratt, *Russian Metaphysical Romanticism: The Poetry of Tiutchev and Boratynskii* (Stanford, Calif., 1984), pp. 42–43.

46. For one discussion of a specific connection between romantic literature and romantic painting, see Karl Kroeber, *Romantic Landscape Vision: Constable and Wordsworth* (Madison, 1975). Cf. Morse Peckham, *Collected Essays: The Triumph of Romanticism* (Columbia, S.C., 1970), pp. 105–22.

could also reappear in a concentrated and indeed overwhelming and unforget-table form. Fedor Tiutchev (1803–73) was the greatest poet of nature in late romanticism. Isolated as a writer and intellectual but also highly cosmopoli-tan (he knew French not just well but perfectly and as a diplomat spent some twenty years in Germany, mainly in Munich, marrying first a Bavarian lady and after her an Alsatian one), Tiutchev contributed peerless Russian verse to the pantheistic or panentheistic cult of nature. As with Wordsworth, the reaction was direct and deep:

> Как ни гнетет рука судьбины,
> Как ни томит людей обман,
> Как ни браздят чело морщины
> И сердце как ни полно ран;
> Каким бы строгим испытаньям
> Вы ни были подчинены,—
> Что устоит перед дыханьем
> И первой встречею весны![47]

Pratt's unpoetic but exact translation reads:

However much the hand of fate oppresses you, however much the deception of people torments you, however many wrinkles furrow your brow and however full of wounds your heart; however severe the trials to which you have been subjected—what can resist the first breath and the first encounter of spring?[48]

His attitude was unmistakably pantheistic:

> Тени сизые смесились,
> Цвет поблекнул, звук уснул—
> Жизнь, движенье разрешились
> В сумрак зыбкий, в дальний гул . . .
> Мотылька полет незримый
> Слышен в воздухе ночном . . .
> Час тоски невыразимой!
> Всё во мне, и я во всем . . .[49]

Gray blue shadows merged, color faded away, sound fell asleep—life and motion dissolved into the tremulous twilight, into a distant hum . . . The

47. Fedor I. Tiutchev, *Polnoe sobranie sochinenii,* ed. Petr V. Bykov, (St. Petersburg, 1913), p. 96. Russian spelling has been modernized throughout.

48. Pratt, *Russian Metaphysical Romanticism,* pp. 72–73. This is the first of the five stanzas of the poem entitled, appropriately, "Vesna" (Spring).

49. Tiutchev, *Polnoe sobranie sochinenii,* p. 58; ellipses in the original. This is the first stanza of the poem entitled "Sumerki" (Twilight).

invisible flight of a moth is heard in the night air . . . Hour of inexpressible yearning! . . . All is in me and I am in all! . . .[50]

Moreover, well acquainted personally with Schelling[51] and generally at home in the world of German romanticism, Tiutchev at times expressed some of its major aspects perhaps even better than the Germans themselves. Witness:

> Дума за думой, волна за волной—
> Два проявленья стихии одной![52]

The English would read,

> Thought after thought, wave after wave—
> Two manifestations of one element!

Tiutchev's pantheism was as relentless in pursuit as the pantheisms of Wordsworth and Novalis:

> О чем ты воешь, ветр ночной?
> О чем так сетуешь безумно?
> Что значит странный голос твой,
> То глухо жалобный, то шумный?
> Понятным сердцу языком
> Твердишь о непонятной муке—
> И роешь и взрываешь в нем
> Порой неистовые звуки!
>
> О, страшных песен сих не пой
> Про древний хаос, про родимый!
> Как жадно мир души ночной
> Внимает повести любимой!
> Из смертной рвется он груди,
> Он с беспредельным жаждет слиться! . .
> О, бурь заснувших не буди—
> Под ними хаос шевелится! . . .[53]

---

50. Pratt, *Russian Metaphysical Romanticism*, p. 157. The poem ends: "Дай вкусить уничтоженья / С миром дремлющим смемай!" ("Let me taste annihilation / Merge me with the slumbering world!")

51. On Schelling's influence on Tiutchev, see, esp., Wsewolod Setschkareff, *Schellings Einfluss in der russischen Literatur der 20er und 30er Jahre des XIX Jahrhunderts* (Berlin, 1939), esp. pp. 99–106; and Pratt, *Russian Metaphysical Literature*.

52. Tiutchev, *Polnoe sobranie sochinenii*, p. 116. These are the first two lines of the poem entitled "14 iiulia 1851 goda" (July 14, 1851).

53. Ibid., p. 84; ellipses in original.

What are you howling about, night wind? What are you lamenting so
madly? . . . What does your strange voice mean, sometimes hollowly plain-
tive, sometimes loud? In a language comprehensible to the heart you speak
of incomprehensible torment, and you burrow and sometimes set off furious
sound in it! . . .

O, do not sing those terrifying songs of ancient chaos, of native chaos! How
avidly the world of the night soul harkens to its favorite tale! It longs to burst
out of the mortal breast, it thirsts to merge with the infinite! . . . O do not
waken sleeping tempests—beneath them chaos stirs! . . .[54]

And, finally, shortly before the poet's death,

> Природа знать не знает о былом,
> Ей чужды наши призрачные годы,
> И перед ней мы смутно сознаём
> Себя самих—лишь грезою природы.
>
> Поочередно всех своихъ детей,
> Свершающих свой подвиг бесполезный,
> Она равно приветствует своей
> Всепоглощающей и миротворной бездной.[55]

Nature evidently does not know of the past; our spectral years are alien to
her; and before her we are vaguely conscious of our very selves—as only a
dream of nature.

She greets all her children as they accomplish their useless feats, equally, each
in turn, with her omnivorous and pacifying abyss.[56]

Genius, whether that of Wordsworth, Novalis, or Tiutchev, is not reward-
ing material for general schemes and conclusions. In our case, in particular, it
is tempting to note the repeated irruptions of pantheism or panentheism into
great modern European poetry and let it go at that. Nevertheless, there was
apparently some continuity and also some evolution. Although similarities in
the treatment of nature by Tiutchev and by the founders of romanticism were
striking, indeed (more could be emphasized if we considered such issues as
timelessness or the remarkable passivity—even to the point of dissolution or
disappearance—of the author's ego), there were also certain differences. After
all, Tiutchev represented faithfully and brilliantly late romanticism; and that
romanticism, to quote Pratt, "expressed the same belief in a living universe
inhabited by supernatural forces and the same precepts of eternal change and
continuing evolution. But the ideas of darkness, death, and mystic transport,
which had been of only peripheral significance before, now became a central

54. Pratt, *Russian Metaphysical Literature,* p. 161.
55. Tiutchev, *Polnoe sobranie sochinenii,* p. 170. These are the last two stanzas of "Po doroge vo
Vshchizh" (On the Road to Vshchizh).
56. Pratt, *Russian Metaphysical Literature,* p. 43.

concern, and the struggle between terror and ecstasy arising from the apoc-alyptic experience became one of the major themes in late romantic liter-ature."[57] Without endorsing this formulation as it stands (and how could one endorse, for example, the implication that death was peripheral for Novalis?) and suspecting that no entirely satisfactory formulation is possible here, I suggest that what came to be missing increasingly in romanticism was pre-cisely the affirmative quality of the vision of the *Frühromantik* or Wordsworth's spots of time. The ecstasy of fulfillment, overwhelming in Wordsworth and Novalis, could not be found in Tiutchev. Only very occasionally, notably in his sublime depiction of early autumn ("There Is in Early Autumn"), the Russian poet approached something akin to perfect harmony and bliss.

To conclude in Tiutchev's words from "Day and Night":

> На мир таинственный духов,
> Над этой бездной безымянной,
> Покров наброшен златотканный
> Высокой волею богов.
> День—сей блистательный покров—
> День, земнородных оживленье,
> Души болящей исцеленье,
> Друг человеков и богов!
>
> Но меркнет день, настала ночь;
> Пришла—и с мира рокового
> Ткань благодатную покрова,
> Сорвав, отбрасывает прочь . . .
> И бездна нам обнажена
> С своими страхами и мглами,
> И нет преград меж ей и нами:
> Вот отчего нам ночь страшна![58]

Upon the mysterious world of spirits, over the nameless abyss, a shroud of golden cloth has been cast by the lofty will of the gods. Day is this glistening cover—day, the enlivening force of earthly beings, the healing power for the aching soul, the friend of men and gods.

But day darkens—night has fallen; it has come—and from the fatal world it casts away, having torn off, the beneficent cloth of the shroud . . . And the abyss is laid bare to us with its horrors and vapors; and there are no barriers between it and us—that is why night is terrifying to us.[59]

Like the concept of nature, the concept of love provided both some con-tinuity and a major focus of concentration for romanticism. Basic to Chris-tianity and a central element of the original romantic vision, it acquired many

---

57. Ibid., p. 147.
58. Tiutchev, *Polnoe sobranie sochinenii,* p. 97; ellipses in original.
59. Pratt, *Russian Metaphysical Literature,* p. 165.

forms in subsequent romantic thought, literature, and art. Frequently, it came to occupy a dominant position.

Romanticists have been repeatedly charged with a divinization of human love—with making that love the supreme value and arbiter in the universe. According to a hostile critic, "Ils ne surent jamais distinguer l'amour divin de l'amour, tout court"[60] ("They could never distinguish divine love from simply love"). Incorrect—Novalis, Wordsworth, and their associates generally made very poor apostles of love *tout court*—the accusation nevertheless points to the characteristic intermingling of the infinite and the finite in romanticism. And with this intermingling, the domain of love expanded in all directions. It also became more negative—or at least came to incorporate remarkable negative elements and areas. Whatever the problems associated with Sophie or Lucy (or Lucinde for that matter), there was no doubt about the indelible positive quality of their images and essences. Yet Keats wrote a few years later:

> I saw pale kings and princes too,
>   Pale warriors, death-pale were they all,
> They cried—"La Belle Dame sans Merci
>   Hath thee in thrall!"[61]

Once again, the unified and flawless—indeed, seamless—world of Wordsworth and *Frühromantik* could not be recovered. Together with other intellectual and artistic trends, romanticism contributed to the secularization of the concept of love and to its enormous prominence in modern Western culture. The special romantic mark here, as elsewhere, was that certain ambivalence between divine and human, the infinite and the finite—before long, even between good and evil.[62]

Beauty constituted another central concept in romanticism. Belonging, like love, to both the Christian religion and the original romantic vision, it too acquired independent life with the breakdown of that vision and proceeded to develop in different directions. Most of these directions led to

---

60. A. Viatte, *Le Catholicisme chez les romantiques,* (Paris, 1922), p. 167.

61. John Keats, "La Belle Dame Sans Merci: A Ballad," in *The Poetical Works of John Keats,* 2d ed., ed. Heathcote W. Garrod (Oxford, 1958), p. 443. One can, of course, argue for continuity even in this instance and, in particular, urge that Sophie was as absorbing and destructive as anything Keats could imagine—La Belle Dame sans Merci, only more so. But the difference in the tone of the two poets is fundamental and unmistakable. Still, one should also consider Coleridge's influence on Keats, as depicted in, e.g., Richard Holmes, *Coleridge: Early Visions* (London, 1989), pp. 252–53.)

62. Another mark, recurrent in romanticism is the inability to state adequately the author's experience, which extends behind and beyond the words—for example, Wordsworth's effort "to invoke the inexpressible." One logical consequence of such inability is silence (as, for example, in Tiutchev's unforgettable poem "Silentium!"). Tiutchev was one of the greatest poets of late, tragic love, as well as of nature. For a different approach to the romanticists' "silence," see Stephen K. Land, "The Silent *Poet:* An Aspect of Wordsworth's Semantic Theory," *University of Toronto Quarterly* 42, no. 2 (Winter 1973): 157–69.

various forms of aestheticism; and the primacy—sometimes the monopoly—of aesthetic values became the hallmark of much late romanticism and also of its impact on still later periods and movements, for example, the so-called Russian Silver Age. Yet the legacy was, in fact, a more complicated one; and it frequently retained, even if in an attenuated or camouflaged form, something of its original religious, metaphysical, and ethical provenance. Dostoevskii probably meant all of that when he made his celebrated statement that beauty will save the world.

Several romantic trends and points of concentration may be profitably mentioned together (and appropriately next to beauty) because of their unusual similarity or close connections, although they have achieved major independent standing in Western culture. I mean, in particular, the romantic cults of poetry, art, and music and of the poet, the artist, and the musician. Novalis, Wordsworth, Coleridge, and Friedrich Schlegel, separately and jointly, produced the greatest affirmation of the value—indeed, the quasi divinity—of poetry in our civilization. It is noteworthy to what extent that affirmation is still with us, although, of course, fragmented, mixed with other influences and attenuated as a rule. Wackenroder best expressed the original total romantic vision of art and music, although Novalis and Friedrich Schlegel at least shared in that vision and said so. Music, especially, became, with the major exception of England and the United States, the premier romantic art and mode of expression. I already had occasion to refer to its remarkable congruence with pantheism or panentheism by virtue of its setting at naught all restrictions of physical form, place, and (in a sense) even time. Of the other explanations of the prominence of music in romanticism, I might cite, from H. G. Schenk's indictment, the argument that music was the perfect medium for that combined theme of a desperate search for absolute values and near nihilism—extreme emotionalism and avoidance of commitment—which he considered central to romanticism.[63] Interestingly, poetry and music stood very close in the romantic tradition and tended to interpenetrate.

The role of the poet and the artist occupied a central position in all stages of romanticism, although it did not escape change. Its most imposing foundation was not even the sterling value of what true poets, artists, and musicians produced, but the act of artistic creation itself, the pantheistic or panentheistic belief of sharing in divine power, of being God. It was at this point that German idealistic philosophy in general and Fichte's philosophy of the ego in particular was most closely connected with the emergence of romanticism. The poet or the artist was, thus, a demiurge creating the world. That surpassing task could be combined to some extent, anachronistically, with a relatively traditional view of God (as may have been the case with

---

63. Schenk, *Mind of the European Romantics,* pp. 201–32, esp. pp. 231–32. Schenk quotes Lamennais: "Music is the sole art of our epoch because that which is vague and mysterious in it corresponds to that oscillation of souls and indefinable suffering which we all experience" (ibid., p. 232).

Wackenroder): man was doing God's work assigned to him by God. It led to a frantic search for a tenable position by such committed intellectuals as Coleridge and Friedrich Schlegel and eventually to their all-out battle against pantheism. It might go a long way toward explaining the "mystery" of Wordsworth's stance in literature and life and the decades he spent denying his great original poetic vision. It was perhaps at its most obvious and explosive in Novalis; and that is why Novalis has been called, often intuitively, the most romantic of all romanticists. The successors to the early romanticists inherited their problem except that they frequently encountered it in a fragmented and generally less obvious form. Also, as secularization continued, the issue of God changed. If there was no God, one could not be God or even do God's work. This could be considered the ultimate triumph, for man became indisputably the only creator; but it also seemed to turn man into nullity. As with other principal romantic concepts, the relationship of human beings to God and to creativity acquired a negative, or "dark,"[64] side in a substantial body of later romantic culture.

That so-called dark side of romanticism may well be regarded as still another major line of romantic development and romantic concentration. Different from others in that it had not been part of the original romantic vision, it resulted, however, directly and logically from the collapse of that vision. If one failed to be with God and to be God, one fateful—and possibly fated—reaction was to turn against God. And it is this challenge to God that formed part of the inspiration of such magnificent romantic poets as Byron, Vigny, or Lermontov. The romantic image of the demon carried a profound meaning; for demons had been angels, with God, and integral elements of the organic celestial order. After their expulsion from paradise everything was reversed. Symphonic unity became separation and alienation, love became hate, good became evil. As Lermontov (1814–41) declared in his stunning, long poem, "A Demon," which he kept writing and rewriting during most of his brief but brilliantly productive life:

> Я тот, чей взор надежду губит,
> Едва надежда расцветёт,
> Я тот, кого никто не любит
> И всё живущее клянёт.[65]

> I am he, whose gaze destroys hope,
> As soon as hope blooms;
> I am he, whom nobody loves,
> And everything that lives curses.

64. I do not like the common label *dark* for this cluster of negative aspects of romanticism because the night—almost a synonym for dark and darkness—had, as we know, a very rich and important positive meaning for Novalis, Friedrich Schlegel, and even, on some significant occasions, Coleridge—and thus, one can argue, for early romanticism in general.

65. Mikhail I. Lermontov, *Polnoe sobranie sochinenii,* ed. Dmitrii I. Abramovich, vol. 2 (St. Petersburg, 1910), p. 368.

The way was indeed opened for all kinds of darker manifestations in romanticism. Still, it should be noted that rebellion against God was only one path to nihilism within the romantic movement. The fading out of the original romantic vision and the failures to replace it successfully, solidly, and permanently with the various substitutes I have been listing in the last few pages constituted others. The romantic world tended to remain in flux, threatened by accusations of nihilism and especially by nihilism itself.[66]

Other points of romantic interest and concentration, such as the fascination of romanticists with the past or the romantic cult of friendship, could also be profitably discussed. H. G. Schenk, himself a chess player, even dealt with romantic chess in a stimulating manner, as have others. I shall limit myself, however, to the remarks already made regarding the content of romanticism and the relationship of content to the original vision and turn to a few observations concerning structure.

Romantic structure was typically threefold. Moreover, the third stage consisted of a return to the first. Often the pattern has been described as union, separation, and reunion. Yet the third stage, reunion, usually did not mean the exact replay of the initial union but, rather, a union made somehow richer through the experience and the overcoming of the period or stage of separation. In philosophical and historical terms the romanticists frequently defined the third stage as a conscious union in contrast to the original unconscious one, as a fully understood and articulated and therefore stronger condition. It is remarkable to what extent that pattern prevailed throughout romanticism.[67]

Novalis' passionate poetry is principally about the transition from the second into the third stage. Indeed, its stunning fervor consists in the poet already grasping that third stage, the reunion. Both the second and the third stages are thus indelibly present in the verse. But so, at least by implication, is the first: there is no doubt at all that Novalis is returning, that he is coming home—the Russian and Tiutchev's adjective *rodnoi* (one's own, one's native) expresses the relationship better than any English word. Prose makes the pattern more explicit, if less explosive. I already had occasion to refer to the story of Hyacinth and Roseblossom, where the hero leaves an idyllic setting only to return eventually to his beloved (or was it to his own true self?). The pattern could be readily transferred to other realms of discourse.

In 1799 Novalis wrote an essay "Die Christenheit oder Europa" (Christianity or Europe).[68] It began: "Once there were fine, resplendent times when

66. On romanticism and nihilism, see Dieter Arendt, *Der "poetische Nihilismus" in der Romantik: Studien zum Verhältnis von Dichtung und Wirklichkeit in der Frühromantik,* 2 vols. (Tübingen, 1972). Arendt provides a rich and impressive account, although somewhat exaggerated—in particular, because he tends to minimize the affirmative aspects of early romanticism and to equate aestheticism with nihilism.

67. This is, of course, not the same as stating that it prevailed only in romanticism. Again, one thinks first of the Christian background.

68. Novalis, *Novalis,* vol. 2, pp. 732–50. My English translations follow Novalis, *"Hymns to the Night" and Other Selected Writings,* trans. Charles E. Passage (New York, 1960), pp. 45–64.

Europe was a Christian land, when one Christendom occupied this humanly constituted continent. One great common interest united the remotest provinces of this broad spiritual realm. Without great worldly possessions, one Head guided and unified the great political forces."[69] The Holy Father in Rome and his saintly assistants led an integrated society based on faith and childish trust. And—it was Novalis who was writing—"they preached solely love for the holy and wondrously beautiful Lady of Christendom, who, endowed with divine powers, was prepared to rescue any believer from the most dread perils."[70] Unfortunately humankind was not ripe, was not prepared for this mode of existence; and it passed, like first love. Division and strife came to the fore. The Protestants had good reason to fight for the freedom of conscience. They accomplished much that was praiseworthy; they destroyed much that was pernicious. But the result was a split in Christendom, which by its very nature must be one. Also, by turning to the Bible as the new binding force, Luther introduced the worldly discipline of philology into the spiritual domain of religion. Separation, fragmentation, and secularization proceeded apace. In Protestantism itself the original heavenly fire was dimmed by worldly preoccupations. Eventually, in France in particular, such phenomena as the Enlightenment, Robespierre, and theophilantrophy appeared. In the absence of gods, specters ruled. With the French Revolution, Europe was divided and poised for a deadly struggle. Only religion could turn the continent back to peace and worthwhile existence. Happily there began a spiritual and cultural revival in Germany:

> All these things are still only intimations, incoherent and raw, but to the historical eye they give evidence of a universal individuality, a new history, a new mankind, the sweetest embrace of a young and surprised Church and a loving God, and a fervent reception of a new Messiah within its thousand members. Who does not, with sweet shame, feel himself pregnant? The newborn child will be the image of his father, a new Golden Age, with dark and infinite eyes, an age prophetic, a wonder-working, miraculously healing, comforting, and kindling eternal life—a great age of reconciliation, a Savior who, like a good spirit, is at home among men, believed in, though not seen, visible under countless forms to believers, consumed as bread and wine, embraced as a bride, breathed as air, heard as word and song, and with heavenly delight accepted as death into the core of the subsiding body amid the supreme pangs of love.[71]

The three stages in the evolution of Europe were thus medieval Christian unity, postmedieval separation and division, and the coming religious age of reunion and reintegration. Characteristically for romantic thought, there was no clear or convincing explanation of why one stage turned, or was to turn, into another—a lacuna resulting ultimately from the fact that the evolution

69. Ibid., p. 45.
70. Ibid., p. 45.
71. Ibid., p. 58.

was conceived as immanent and therefore not subject to external causes or specific circumstances. Also, the third period, referring invariably to the future and, at best, only in its inception to the present was of necessity vague and speculative in romantic ideology, although often not quite as mystical and fantastic as in the case of Novalis. Friedrich Schlegel, for his part, based much of his historical thinking on a scheme very similar to his friend's, except that his favorite stages were the harmony of antiquity, the disharmony of modernity, and the coming era of harmony. Indeed, it is difficult to deal with romantic ideology to any extent without encountering this tripartite dialectic. We shall meet it next (and repeatedly) in discussing the romantic concept of *organicism*.

Organicism was probably the most important single concept in the structuring of romantic thought. I would suggest that its deep foundation and strength resided in pantheism or panentheism, which can be considered the epitome of a unified organic world. Once the total vision broke down, more limited substitute organisms came to the fore. They had to be substitutes because the original all-inclusive vision (Wordsworth's spots of time or Novalis' ecstatic longing for absorption into the night, death, and love) left no room for the worship of the Middle Ages or for integral nationalism. Even more to the point, the original experience was on a much more primitive and profound level than society, politics, or economics; and only with its passing could it—or bits of it—be adjusted to more mundane subjects. For that reason, romanticists could be reactionary or radical, champions or sworn foes of the pope and the Jesuits, defenders or enemies of the Austrian or the Russian empires. What made them romantic belonged to a different order of reality. But in any case, once the floodgates were opened, the substitute organisms of all kinds rushed forth in a bewildering variety of patterns. I shall use as illustration the Slavophile pattern, because I know it best.[72] In addition, it is a remarkably rich and authentic romantic ideology.

The Slavophiles were a group of Russian romantic intellectuals who formulated a comprehensive and noteworthy ideology centered on their belief in the superior nature and supreme historical mission of Orthodoxy and of Russia. The leading members of the group—all of them landlords and gentleman–scholars of broad culture and many intellectual interests—included Alexis Khomiakov, who applied himself to everything from theology and world history to medicine and technical inventions; Ivan Kireevskii, who has been called the philosopher of the movement; his brother Peter, who collected folk songs and left very little behind him in writing; Constantine Aksakov, a specialist in Russian history and language; Constantine's brother Ivan, later prominent as a publicist and a Pan-Slav; and George Samarin, who was to have a significant part in the emancipation of the serfs and who wrote especially on certain religious and philosophical topics, on the problem of the

---

72. My most comprehensive treatment of Slavophilism remains my first published piece on the subject, *Russia and the West in the Teaching of the Slavophiles: A Study of Romantic Ideology* (Cambridge, Mass., 1952).

borderlands of the empire, and on the issue of reform in Russia. One could refer to a distinct Slavophile ideology from 1839. The informal group, gathering in the salons and the homes of Moscow, where its members engaged for a number of years in a running debate with their celebrated opponents, the Westernizers, flourished in the 1840s and 1850s until the death of the Kireevskii brothers in 1856 and of Khomiakov and Constantine Aksakov in 1860. As well-educated intellectuals and late romanticists, the Slavophiles knew foreign languages well, traveled and occasionally studied in Europe outside Russia, and generally showed great interest in European intellectual life, some of them counting Schelling and other Western luminaries as their personal acquaintances. They were especially influenced by German idealistic philosophy.

Slavophilism expressed a fundamental vision of integration, peace, and harmony among men. On the religious plane it produced Khomiakov's concept of *sobornost,* an association in love, freedom, and truth of Christian believers, which Khomiakov considered the essence of Orthodoxy.[73] Historically (so the Slavophiles asserted) a similar harmonious integration of individuals could be found in the social life of the Slavs, notably in the peasant commune. Indeed, the entire pre-Petrine history of Russia was a study in organic integration: the state had been formed by the people inviting princes to rule, not by conquest; there was no internal division, struggle, or violence but rather the happy life of a united society; and the true Orthodox religion bestowed its priceless benefits on all the Russians. Even the Russian language was the most organic of all the languages.[74] As against this realm of love, freedom, and cooperation stood the world of rationalism, necessity, and compulsion. It, too, existed on many planes, from the religious and metaphysical to that of everyday life. Thus, it manifested itself in the Roman Catholic church (which had chosen rationalism and authority in preference to love and harmony and had seceded from Orthodox Christendom) and, through the Catholic church, in Protestantism and in the entire civilization of the West. Most important, Peter the Great introduced the principles of rationalism, legalism, and compulsion into Russia, where they proceeded to destroy or stunt the harmonious native development and to seduce the educated public. The future of Russia lay clearly in a return to native principles, in overcoming the Western disease. After being cured, Russia would take its message of harmony and salvation to the discordant and dying West. As a

---

73. See my "Khomiakov on *Sobornost',*" in *Continuity and Change in Russian and Soviet Thought,* ed. by Ernest J. Simmons (Cambridge, Mass., 1955), where I try to analyze the dual origin of the concept in romanticism and in the Orthodox tradition and assign a certain priority to romanticism. See also my "A. S. Khomiakov's Religious Thought," *St. Vladimir's Theological Quarterly* 23, no. 2 (1979): 87–100.

74. To quote Constantine Aksakov: "Indeed, the Russian word is not some chance growing together of the national essences with different principles and characters (as, for instance, are the French, Italian, and English languages) but a living expression of original and independent thought; it is no more possible to tell a Russian, 'Speak thus' than it is to tell him 'Think thus'" (*Polnoe sobranie sochinenii,* [Moscow, 1961–80], vol. 3, p. 197).

student of romanticism will readily recognize, the all-embracing Slavophile dichotomy represented the basic romantic contrast between the romantic ideal and the Age of Reason, except that Russia became the ideal and the West its opposite.[75]

The three-stage dialectic structured and permeated the Slavophile teaching. The two main sequences may be designated as the religious and the Russian-historical, which came to be regarded as the quintessence of Slavophilism; but there were also others, often subsidiary to the principal two. The religious dialectic went from Christian unity to the tragic division produced by the willful Roman Catholic secession and on to a reunion in the future.[76] The Russian-historical dialectic had as its three stages the original organic Russia, its destruction by Peter the Great, and its coming rebirth at a still higher (because more conscious) level.[77]

Throughout the Slavophile ideology the organic, unifying, and integrative principles and qualities occupied the positive pole as against everything mechanistic, divisive, and fragmenting. The immanent tended to have precedence over the transcendent. A. S. Khomiakov defined the church as follows:

No! The Church is not authority, just as God is not authority, just as Christ is not authority—because authority is something external to us. Not authority, I say, but truth and at the same time the life of a Christian, his inner life; for God, Christ, the Church live in him a life which is more real than the

75. To the best of my knowledge this point was first made fully and explicitly by F. A. Stepun, "Nemetskii romantizm i russkoe slavianofilstvo," *Russkaia mysl,* March 1910, esp. pp. 73–75. Cf. Stepun's later article "Deutsche Romantik und die Geschichtsphilosophie der Slawophilen," *Logos* (1927): 46–67. Important recent Western studies of the Slavophiles include Peter K. Christoff, *An Introduction to Nineteenth-Century Russian Slavophilism: A Study in Ideas,* 4 vols. (The Hague, 1961, 1972; Princeton, N.J., 1982; Boulder, 1991) and Andrzej Walicki, *The Slavophile Controversy: History of a Conservative Utopia in Nineteenth Century Russian Thought* (Oxford, 1975). For the Soviet scene, see my *Recent Soviet Scholarship on the Slavophiles.* Bernard Moses Memorial Lecture, no. 30 (Berkeley, 1985).

76. The issue of unity and separation—so emotionally, as well as intellectually, central to romanticism—is marvelously presented in Khomiakov's fictitious account of an Orthodox traveler in Western lands who, when he hears the addition of *filioque* to the Creed in the liturgy, discovers that the West had split from Christendom. (*Polnoe sobranie sochinenii* [Moscow, 1990–1914], vol. 2, pp. 48–49. It is interesting that both Coleridge and Friedrich Schlegel considered *filioque* an important issue and championed the Western position against the Orthodox. See McFarland, *Romanticism,* p. 375, n. 67, and Imle, *Schlegels Entwicklung,* p. 217.

77. As an example of a "subsidiary" dialectic supporting this principal one, take Ivan Aksakov's treatment of the two great Russian cities—the historic Moscow and the new Petrine and Western St. Petersburg: "St. Petersburg as the embodiment of a negative moment of history cannot create anything *positive* in the Russian sense. According to a well-known dialectical law, it is possible to return to *the positive* only through *a negation of the negation itself,* in other words through a negation of the St. Petersburg period, through a negation of St. Petersburg as a political *principle* which guided Russian life for almost two centuries. The result will be a Russian nation freed from exclusiveness and called into the arena of world history. Is that clear?" (*Sochineniia* [Moscow, 1886–91], vol. 5, p. 632).

Obviously, the capital had to be returned back to Moscow. On the Slavophile evaluation of Peter the Great, see my *Image of Peter the Great in Russian History and Thought* (New York, 1985), pp. 142–51.

heart which beats in his breast or the blood which flows in his veins; but they live in him only inasmuch as he himself lives an ecumenical life of love and unity, that is, the life of the Church.[78]

Following the central Christian theological tradition in what it fundamentally asserted, this and other such statements nevertheless worried the Orthodox authorities because of what they did not say, namely, that the church (or that God for that matter) is present outside the believer—just as very similar liberal Catholic formulations worry the Vatican at present.[79]

Organicism also became the measure of human institutions. The Slavophiles glorified the family. They naturally preferred custom and tradition to legislative enactments;[80] in fact, few concepts were as repellent to them as that of the abstract legal mind shaping life and society according to its own dictates. And (as already indicated) they emphasized the organic nature of Russian history and Russian social institutions. For a single example, consider Constantine Aksakov's affirmation of the Russian peasant commune:

> A commune is a union of the people who have renounced their egoism, their individuality, and who express their common accord; this is an act of love, a noble Christian act, which expresses itself more or less clearly in its various other manifestations. A commune thus represents a moral choir; and just as in a choir a voice is not lost but follows the general pattern and is heard in the harmony of all voices, so in the commune the individual is not lost but renounces his exclusiveness in favor of a general accord—and there arises the noble phenomenon of a harmonious, joint existence of rational beings (consciousness); there arises a brotherhood, a commune—a triumph of human spirit.[81]

As Nicholas Berdiaev commented: "The Slavophiles were under the influence of their *narodnik* illusions. To them the commune was not a fact of history, but something imposing which stands outside the realm of history; it is the 'other world' so to speak within this world."[82]

The Slavophile projection of Russia to center stage was one of the very many adoptions and adaptations of romanticism to serve nationalistic purposes. Needless to say, in their case (as in the great majority of other cases) the

78. Khomiakov, *Polnoe sobranie sochinenii,* vol. 2, p. 53.

79. The striking resemblance, to be sure, is a result not of Khomiakov's influence, direct or indirect, but of the same rich Christian, and perhaps romantic, tradition.

80. Khomiakov writes: "Law and custom rule the social life of the peoples. Law, written and armed with compulsion, brings the differing private wills into a conditional unity. Custom, unwritten and unarmed, is the expression of the most basic unity of society. It is as closely connected with the personality of a people as the habits of life are connected with the personality of a man. The broader the sphere of custom, the stronger and healthier the society and the richer and more original the development of its jurisprudence" (*Polnoe sobranie sochinenii,* vol. 3, p. 75).

81. Konstantin Aksakov, *Sochineniia istoricheskie* (Moscow, 1861), pp. 291–92. Compare the subsequent fortunes of the concept of the peasant commune in Russian history.

82. Nikolai A. Berdyaev, *The Russian Idea* (London, 1947), p. 50.

substitution was sincere. Indeed, whereas the original romantic vision embraced the universe in enormous exultation and tension, the nationalist surrogate was much more realistic and manageable; yet it still provided a basis for belonging, loyalty, devotion, even heroic devotion, and organic integration. Language, so important for romanticism and also for nationalism, seemed to confirm the validity of the organic view of the world; for assuredly, languages were functions of national or ethnic organisms and not creatures of abstract reason, individual effort, or adventitious circumstances. The ego, which once aimed to encompass all and merge with God (perhaps better, to be God), retained its high ambition but now limited to the national, ethnic or racial organism. Poets, philosophers, artists, and even statesmen came to be conceived of as the true expressions—even incarnations—of their respective organisms. Apolitical or prepolitical in its essence, romanticism proved to be extremely adaptable to political and historical conditions. If in Russia Slavophile romanticism was one of the reactions of a conservative society to modernization, in Poland (for instance) romanticism played a much more radical and valiant role.[83] All in all, it is entirely possible that it is through its impact on nationalism that romanticism has exercised its greatest influence in the modern world.

But such things cannot be measured. And I certainly would not want to argue that nationalism was simply a result of romanticism. One can only note that romanticism did have a part in the rise of nationalism, as it did in other important nineteenth- and twentieth-century developments. For example, what, exactly, was its contribution to the evolution of individualism, subjectivism, and existentialism? When does romanticism stop being romanticism and become something else? Issues acquire additional complexity when value judgments enter the assessment. Appropriately, among books on romanticism and its fortunes, are found both F. L. Lucas's *Decline and Fall of the Romantic Ideal* and Morse Peckham's *Triumph of Romanticism*.

III

Some concluding remarks are in order. I approached the problem of the emergence of romanticism with the assumption that such an emergence did

---

83. On Polish romanticism, see, esp., Andrzej Walicki, *Philosophy and Romantic Nationalism: The Case of Poland* (Oxford, 1982), and, most recently, Jerzy Jedlicki, "Holy Ideals and Prosaic Life; or, The Devil's Alternatives," in *Polish Paradoxes,* ed. Stanislaw Gomulka and Antony Polonsky (New York, 1990), pp. 40–62. A minor study in romantic "adaptability" is my "On Lammenais, Chaadaev, and the Romantic Revolt in France and Russia," *American Historical Review* 82, no. 5 (Dec. 1977): 1165–86. On the development of the romantic classification of peoples, see Hugo Moser, "Der Stammesgedanke im Schrifttum der Romantik und bei Ludwig Uhland (eine Studie)," in *Festschrift Paul Kluckhohn und Hermann Schneider gewidmet zu ihrem 60. Geburtstag* (Tübingen, 1948). The latest joint volume on the nature and fortunes of romanticism in different European countries (in this case thirteen, although one is Scandinavia, and another Wales) is Roy Porter and Mikulas Teich, ed., *Romanticism in National Context* (New York, 1988). (Donald Pirie's contribution, "The Agony in the Garden: Polish Romanticism," presents starkly the crucial role of romanticism in Polish history.)

occur and tried to identify its location in place, time, and provenance and its nature. In other words, I see intellectual and cultural history as proceeding in bursts (sometimes as in this case very significant bursts) rather than as a seamless pattern. While I suspect that my education, aesthetic tastes, and other subjective factors contributed to this point of view, I would still defend it in terms of its correspondence to reality, imperfect though my argument is bound to be philosophically.[84]

However, my tying the appearance of romanticism strictly to the late 1790s does not necessarily eliminate or even diminish the importance for my topic of the preceding decades and centuries and the scholarship devoted to them. To underline the obvious, if pantheism or panentheism was crucial to the emergence of romanticism, its presence and evolution in Europe acquires central significance. And that issue alone appears to range from neo-Platonists and Spinoza to Böhme, the hermeticists and the Unitarians, as well as many others. But connections do not have to be direct and (so to speak) linear. For romanticism to emerge, the stage had to be set. To illustrate what that meant (one example among many), M. H. Abrams (in his first major book on romanticism, *The Mirror and the Lamp*) and other scholars have traced a fundamental evolution in eighteenth-century Europe from content-centered and, in part, public-centered literature to author-centered literature. The author finally came to the fore. Without that prior development, I find it impossible to imagine romanticism.

Predecessors and older contemporaries of the early romanticists included such imposing figures as Blake in England, Rousseau in France (or Switzerland), and Goethe and Schiller in Germany. In Germany in particular they included whole major schools and movements, (notably Sturm und Drang), and entire generations of writers. While all these were still not romanticists proper by most definitions (including mine), they enriched immeasurably and often relevantly for my purposes the intellectual and cultural scene.

German idealistic philosophers were of special significance. Two of them at least, Fichte and Schelling, made different, but certainly major, contributions to romanticism and are frequently listed as romanticists. Fichte, more than anyone else, provided with his doctrine of the ego the basic philosophy for *Frühromantik*. Schelling covered very much romantic ground, including pantheism itself. Interestingly, in terms of personal evolution, his life broke into two parts like Friedrich Schlegel's (and Coleridge's and Wordsworth's) and at about the same time, around the year 1806. He, too, moved from pantheism toward a more traditional theism and with it to a more pessimistic and conservative outlook on life. Many specialists believe that he, too, lost his inspiration and creativity. It is only because of my narrow focus on the

---

84. I have long been intrigued by the problem of intellectual origins. See, esp., my "Emergence of Eurasianism," *California Slavic Studies* 4(1967): 39–72.

original romantic vision that I decided not to deal with German idealistic philosophy and with such issues as whether absolute idealism implies or overlaps with pantheism. A broader definition of romanticism would make room for German idealistic philosophy.

I have also been very exclusive in regard to unmistakable romanticists. My focus, of course, limited me to early romanticism—even to the point of stressing its difference from what came later—largely disregarding the subsequent course of the sweeping romantic movement in general. Still, my narrow selection can certainly be challenged. Thus, I decided that Hölderlin, although extremely interesting and in a number of ways parallel to what I have been discussing, nevertheless did not belong to my group. Thematically and in terms of his own inspiration, I also ruled out Kleist, although he was only a few years younger than my protagonists and brilliantly similar to them in certain respects (notably to Novalis on the subject of the cult of death). Other scholars could judge and have judged otherwise.[85] Even in the core German early romantic cluster I did discuss, I paid no attention to August Wilhelm Schlegel or to Tieck. Here I tend to agree with Walter Silz, who wrote: "August Wilhem Schlegel was not a Romanticist at heart, but a skilful lecturer who popularized and disseminated the Romantic ideas that originated chiefly in his brother's profound and fertile brain. Tieck was a born actor, who with fine adaptability played a Romantic role during one period of his varied career."[86] The last, to be sure, is a serious accusation and needs much more study than what I accorded it; but it finds support in Friedrich Schlegel, as well as in later scholarship. Schleiermacher's proved to be the most difficult case. Very close to Friedrich Schlegel and Novalis in his first "intuitive-creative" (*intuitive-schöpferische*) period of intellectual activity, 1796–1802,[87] Schleiermacher apparently affected his romanticist friends deeply. He has even been cited, both together with Fichte and separately, as the main source for romantic ideology: Fichte in philosophy, Schleiermacher in religion and ethics. He won and has maintained great fame as the romanticist theologian. But this might well be just the point. A Christian theologian from the beginning and never abandoning that position, Schleiermacher could not share in pantheism/panentheism or self-divinization, which I regard as the igniting romantic spark. Not surprisingly, he argued as often against his romanticist

85. For example, "Heinrich von Kleist, though he came into immediate contact only with later Romanticists, is to be numbered, by right of personal and poetic character as well as of historical position, with the originators of Romanticism" (Walter Silz, *Early German Romanticism, Its Founders and Heinrich von Kleist* [Cambridge, Mass., 1929], p. ix).

86. Ibid., p. 20. As Karin Thornton put it in regard to the celebrated collaboration between Tieck and Wackenroder, "Wackenroder appears as the leading spirit, while Tieck is the follower and imitator" ("Wackenroder's Objective Romanticism," *Germanic Review* 37 [May 1962]: 168).

87. The periodization and the terminology are from Martin Redeker, *Friedrich Schleiermacher: Leben und Werk (1768 bis 1834)* (Berlin, 1968), p. 11. The most important texts are Schleiermacher's *Über die Religion: Reden an die Gebildeten unter ihren Verächtern* ([Berlin,] 1979) and *Monologen* ([Berlin,] 1800), as well as his correspondence during this period.

friends as with them or for them.[88] For England, the problem of inclusion was rather easily resolved. I gave some thought to Southey but decided in the negative.

Historians often move from personal and intellectual relations among individuals to huge general topics, and vice versa, because both kinds of phenomena play their parts in the lives of men and women. My present intention is merely to mention a few of these major events and developments and to indicate that I am not unaware of them. Traditionally, the great French Revolution (and perhaps its failure compared to the expectations) has been posited as at least one of the reasons for the emergence of romanticism. Some time ago I would have accepted without reservation such a bald statement, as well as the contrasting exposition of the doctrines of the Enlightenment and of the French Revolution on the one hand and romantic ideology on the other that frequently follows. But the issue is more complex. For one thing, certain protoromantic doctrines (such as that of the living universe) were linked with radicalism and revolution (where Wordsworth and Coleridge found them) rather than the reaction against revolution. More important, the original romantic vision was apart from rather than against the French Revolution. As I have emphasized, it took effect on a more primitive and deeper level than politics. One had to be ready for the vision; and in that sense enthusiasm for and disappointment in the French Revolution and, to some extent, in reason itself might have been exactly the preparation needed. Characteristically, the men who created early romanticism had abandoned, or were in the process of abandoning, various political and rationalistic beliefs. Possibly a certain vacuum had to be established. But there was not, and could not be, any balance (antithetical or otherwise) between the Convention and Robespierre, on the one side, and Novalis' absorption into the night and Wordsworth's into nature, on the other. Later rich and elaborate romantic teachings presented symmetrical challenges to the philosophy of the Age of Reason and closely argued refutations of the French Revolution, but they cannot serve as guides to the emergence of romanticism.

As regards German history, the destruction of Prussia by Napoleon in 1806 and the subsequent Prussian (and eventually German) national revival have been cited as of decisive importance for romanticism as for much else. The battle of Jena and the reaction to it marked the divide between the aesthetic, humanistic, and individualistic *Frühromantik* and the later romantic nationalism. That formulation, to be sure, tells us much more about the second and following phases of German romanticism (I stressed how well organic romanticism suited nationalist beliefs) than about its origins. As for Russia, we are taken back to the significance of the westernization of that country, associated especially with Peter the Great and the century which

88. His focus more precise and narrow, Alfred Schlagdenhauffen argued that Schleiermacher broke with Friedrich Schlegel and his circle because he refused to integrate religion with poetry and "plastic visions" (*Frédéric Schlegel et son groupe: La doctrine de l'Athenaeum [1798–1800]* [Paris, 1934], p. 365).

followed his reign; for without it there would have been no contributions to romanticism by Tiutchev, Lermontov, the Slavophiles, or other Russians.

My search has been narrow and, perhaps, deceptive. History is a story of change and multiple causation. It may be quixotic to look for the first inspiration and try to trace it and its results in later years. Yet it is when dealing with original ideas or perceptions and genuine poetry that this approach appears at times to impose itself. It was Boris Pasternak who wrote, "The clearest, the most memorable, and the most important point in art is its emergence; and the greatest works of art of the world are, in fact, while narrating about most diverse things, telling of their own birth."[89]

89. Boris Pasternak, *Avtobiografischeskii ocherk: Proza* (Ann Arbor, Mich., 1961), p. 241.

Works Cited

Abrams, M. H. *The Mirror and the Lamp: Romantic Theory and the Critical Tradition.* New York, 1953.

———. "Structure and Lyric in Greater Romantic Style." In *From Sensibility to Romanticism: Essays Presented to Frederick A. Pottle,* ed. Frederick W. Hillers and Harold Bloom. New York, 1965.

———. *Natural Supernaturalism: Tradition and Revolution in Romantic Literature.* New York, 1971.

Aksakov, Konstantin. *Polnoe sobranie sochinenii.* 3 vols. Moscow, 1861–80.

———. *Sochineniia istoricheskie.* Moscow, 1861.

Anderson, Eugene N. "German Romanticism as an Ideology of Cultural Crisis." *Journal of the History of Ideas* 2, no. 3 (June 1941): 301–17.

Arendt, Dieter. *Der "poetische Nihilismus" in der Romantik: Studien zum Verhätlnis von Dichtung und Wirklichkeit in der Frühromantik.* 2 vols. Tübingen, 1972.

Athenaeum (Berlin) 1–3 (1798–1800).

Averill, James H. *Wordsworth and the Poetry of Human Suffering.* Ithaca, N.Y., 1980.

Babbitt, Irving. *Rousseau and Romanticism.* Boston, 1919.

Bald, R. C. "Coleridge and 'The Ancient Mariner': Addenda to *The Road to Xanadu.*" In *Nineteenth-Century Studies,* ed. Herbert Davis, William C. Devane, and R. C. Bald. Ithaca, N.Y., 1940.

Barfield, Owen. *What Coleridge Thought.* Middletown, Conn., 1971.

Barth, J. Robert. *Coleridge and Christian Doctrine.* Cambridge, Mass., 1969.

Bate, Walter Jackson. *Coleridge.* London, 1968.

Bateson, F. W. *Wordsworth: A Re-interpretation.* London, 1956.

Beer, J. B. *Coleridge the Visionary.* London, 1959.

Behler, Ernst. "Der Wendepunkt Friedrich Schlegels: Ein Bericht über unveröffentliche Schriften F. Schlegels in Köln und Trier." In *Romantikforschung seit 1945,* ed. Klaus Peter. Königstein, 1980.

———. *Friedrich Schlegel in Selbstzeugnissen und Bilddokumenten.* Hamburg, 1966.

Bostetter, Edward. *The Romantic Ventriloquists: Wordsworth, Coleridge, Keats, Shelley, Byron.* Seattle, Wash., 1963.

Boulger, James D. *Coleridge as Religious Thinker.* New Haven, Conn., 1961.

Bowra, C. M. *The Romantic Imagination.* New York, 1961.

Brett, R. L. and A. R. Jones. Introduction to the *Lyrical Ballads, by William Wordsworth and Samuel Taylor Coleridge. The text of the 1798 edition with the additional 1800 poems and the Prefaces.* Ed. R. L. Brett and A. R. Jones. London, 1963.

Brooks, Cleanth. *The Well Wrought Urn: Studies in the Structure of Poetry.* New York, 1947.

———. "Wordsworth and Human Suffering: Notes on Two Early Poems." in *From Sensibility to Romanticism: Essays Presented to Frederick A. Pottle.* ed. Frederick W. Hillers and Harold Bloom. New York, 1965.

Brown, Marshall. *The Shape of German Romanticism.* Ithaca, N.Y., 1959.

Campbell, Oscar James, and Paul Mueschke. " 'Guilt and Sorrow': A Study in the Genesis of Wordsworth's Aesthetic." *Modern Philology* 23 (1925/26): 293–306.

Christoff, Peter K. *An Introduction to Nineteenth-Century Russian Slavophilism: A Study in Ideas.* Vol. 1: *A. S. Xomjakov.* The Hague, 1961.

———. *An Introduction to Nineteenth-Century Russian Slavophilism: A Study in Ideas.* Vol. 2: *I. V. Kireevskij.* The Hague, 1972.

———. *An Introduction to Nineteenth-Century Russian Slavophilism: A Study in Ideas.* Vol. 3: *K. S. Aksakov.* Princeton, N.J., 1982.

———. *An Introduction to Nineteenth-Century Russian Slavophilism: A Study in Ideas.* Vol. 4. *Iu. F. Samarin.* Boulder, Colo., 1991.

Coleridge, Samuel Taylor. *Biographia Literaria; or, Biographical Sketches of My Literary Life and Opinions.* Ed. George Watson. London, 1960.

———. *Coleridge: Poetical Works.* Ed. Ernest Hartley Coleridge. Oxford, 1969.

———. *Collected Letters of Samuel Taylor Coleridge.* 6 vols. Ed. Earl Leslie Griggs. Oxford, 1956–71.

Cooke, Michael G. "The Manipulation of Space in Coleridge's Poetry." In *New Perspectives on Coleridge and Wordsworth: Selected Papers from the English Institute,* ed. Geoffrey H. Hartman. New York, 1972.

Cornwell, Neil. *The Life, Times, and Milieu of V. F. Odoyevsky, 1804–1869.* Athens, Ohio, 1986.

Danby, John F. *The Simple Wordsworth: Studies in the Poems, 1797–1807.* London, 1960. (Reprinted 1968, 1971).

Deutschbein, Max. *Das Wesen des Romantischen.* Göthen, 1921.

Dickey, Lawrence. *Hegel: Religion, Economics, and the Politics of the Spirit, 1770–1807.* New York, 1987.

Eichner, Hans. "The Genesis of German Romanticism." *Queens' Quarterly* 72, no. 2 (Summer 1965): 213–31.

Evans, B. Ifor. "Wordsworth and the European Problem of the Twentieth Century." In *Wordsworth Centenary Studies Presented at Cornell and Princeton Universities,* ed. Gilbert T. Dunklin. Princeton, N.J., 1951.

Ferguson, Frances. *Wordsworth: Language as Counter-Spirit.* New Haven, Conn., 1977.

Ferry, David. *The Limits of Mortality: An Essay on Wordsworth's Major Poems.* Middleton, Conn., 1959.

Forstman, Jack. *Romantic Triangle: Schleirmacher and Early German Romanticism.* Missoula, Mont., 1977.

Frank, Manfred. *Das Problem "Zeit" in der deutschen Romantik: Zeitbewusstsein und Bewusstsein von Zeitlichkeit in der frühromantischen Philosophie und in Tiecks Dichtung.* Munich, 1972.

Fricke, Gerhard. "Bemerkungen zu Wilhelm Heinrich Wackenroders Religion der Kunst." In *Festschrift Paul Kluckhon und Hermann Schneider gewidmet zu ihren 60. Geburstag.* Tübingen, 1948.

Gabitova, R. M. *Filosofiia nemetskogo romantizma.* Moscow, 1978.

Gill, Stephen. *William Wordsworth: A Life.* Oxford, 1989.

Griggs, Earl Leslie. "Wordsworth Through Coleridge's Eyes." In *Wordsworth Centenary Studies Presented at Cornell and Princeton Universities,* ed. Gilbert T. Dunklin. Princeton, N.J., 1951.

Grob, Alan *The Philosophic Mind: A Study of Wordsworth's Poetry and Thought, 1797–1805.* Columbus, Ohio, 1973.

Harper, George McLean, *William Wordsworth: His Life, Works, and Influence.* 2 vols. 1929. Reprint. New York, 1960.

Hartman, Geoffrey H. "Reflections on the Evening Star: Akenside to Coleridge." In *New Perspectives on Coleridge and Wordsworth. Selected Papers from the English Institute.* ed. Geoffrey H. Hartman. New York, 1972.

———. *The Unmediated Vision: An Interpretation of Wordsworth, Hopkins, Rilke, and Valéry.* New York, 1966.

Haven, Richard. *Patterns of Consciousness: An Essay on Coleridge.* Amherst, Mass., 1969.

Heffernan, James. *Wordsworth's Theory of Poetry: The Transforming Imagination.* Ithaca, N.Y. 1969.

Hiebel, Friedrich. *Novalis: Deutscher Dichter, europäischer Denker, christlicher Seher.* 2d ed. Bern, 1972.

Holmes, Richard. *Coleridge.* Past Masters Series. Oxford, 1982.

———. *Coleridge: Early Visions.* London, 1989.

Imle, F. *Friedrich von Schlegels [religiöse] Entwicklung von Kant zum Katholizismus.* Paderborn, 1927.

Jacobus, Mary. *Romanticism, Writing, and Sexual Differences: Essays on "The Prelude."* Oxford, 1989.

Jedlicki, Jerzy. "Holy Ideals and Prosaic Life; or, The Devil's Alternatives." In *Polish Paradoxes,* ed. Stanislaw Gomulka and Antony Polonsky. New York, 1990.

Joachim, Marie. *Die Weltanschauung der Romantik.* Jena, 1905.

Jordan, John E. *Why the Lyrical Ballads? The Background, Writing, and Character of Wordsworth's 1798 "Lyrical Ballads."* Berkeley, Calif., 1976.

Keats, John. "La Belle Dame sans Merci: A Ballad." In *The Poetical Works of John Keats,* 2d ed., ed. H. W. Garrod, Oxford, 1958.

Khomiakov, A. S. *Polnoe sobranie sochinenii.* 8 vols. Moscow, 1900–1914.

Kluckhohn, Paul. *Das Ideengut der deutschen Romantik.* Tübingen, 1953.

———. *Persönlichkeit und Gemeinschaft: Studien zur Staatsauffassung der deutschen Romantik.* Halle, 1925.

Kohlschmidt, Werner. "Der Wortschatz der Innerlichkeit bei Novalis." *Festschrift Paul Kluckhohn und Hermann Schneider gewidmet zu ihrem 60. Geburstag.* Tübingen, 1948.

Korff, H. A. *Geist der Goethezeit: Versuch einer ideellen Entwicklung der klassisch–romantischen Literaturgeschichte.* Vol. 3: *Frühromantik.* Leipzig, 1957.

———. *Geist der Goethezeit: Versuch einer ideellen Entwicklung der klassisch-romantischen Literaturgeschichte.* Vol. IV: *Hochromantik.* Leipzig, 1956.

Kroeber, Karl. *Romantic Landscape Vision: Constable and Wordsworth.* Madison, Wisc., 1975.

Land, Stephen K. "The Silent *Poet:* An Aspect of Wordsworth's Semantic Theory." *University of Toronto Quarterly,* 42, no. 2 (Winter 1973): 157–69.

La Vopa, Anthony J. *Grace, Talent, and Merit: Poor Students, Clerical Careers, and Professional Ideology in Eighteenth-Century Germany.* New York, 1988.

Lermontov, M. Iu. *Polnoe sobranie sochinenii.* 5 vols. Ed. D. I. Abramovich, St. Petersburg, 1910.

Lindenberger, Herbert. *On Wordsworth's "Prelude."* Princeton, N.J., 1963.

Lipking, Lawrence, ed. *High Romantic Argument: Essays for M. H. Abrams.* Ithaca, N.Y., 1981.

Lockridge, Lawrence S. *Coleridge the Moralist.* Ithaca, N.Y., 1977.

Lovejoy, Arthur O. "On the Discrimination of Romanticisms." In *Essays in the History of Ideas.* Baltimore, Md., 1948.

Lowes, John Livingston, *The Road to Xanadu: A Study in the Ways of the Imagination.* Boston, 1927.

Lussky, Alfred Edwin. *Tieck's Romantic Irony, with Special Emphasis upon the Influence of Cervantes, Sterne, and Goethe.* Chapel Hill, N.C., 1932.

McEldery, B. R., Jr., "Coleridge's Revision of the 'The Ancient Mariner'." *Studies in Philology* 29 (1932): 68–94.

McFarland, Thomas. *Coleridge and the Pantheist Tradition.* Oxford, 1962.

———. *Romanticism and the Forms of Ruin: Wordsworth, Coleridge, and Modalities of Fragmentation.* Princeton, N.J., 1981.

McGann, Jerome J. "The Meaning of the Ancient Mariner." *Critical Inquiry,* 8, no. 1 (Autumn 1981): 35–67.

———. *The Romantic Ideology: A Critical Investigation.* Chicago, 1983.

Mähl, Hans-Joachim. *Die Idee des goldenen Zeitalters im Werk des Novalis.* Heidelberg, 1965.

Mann, Otto. *Der junge Friedrich Schlegel: Eine Analyse von Existenz und Werk.* Berlin, 1932.

Margouliouth, H. M. *Wordsworth and Coleridge—1795–1834.* London, 1955.

Martin, Alfred von. "Romantische Konversionen." *Logos* 17 (1928): 141–64.

Menhennet, Alan. *The Romantic Movement.* Totowa, N.J., 1981.

Miller, John T., Jr. "Private Faith and Public Religion: S. T. Coleridge's Confrontation with Secularism." In *The Secular Mind: Transformations of Faith in Modern Europe.* Ed. W. Warren Wagar. New York, 1982.

Moorman, Mary. *William Wordsworth: A Biography.* Vol. 1: *The Early Years, 1770–1803.* Oxford, 1957.

Moser, Hugo. "Der Stammesgedanke im Schriftum der Romantik und bei Ludwig Uhland (eine Studie)." In *Festschrift Paul Kluckhohn und Hermann Schneider gewidmet zu ihrem 60. Geburtstag.* Tübingen, 1948.

Muirhead, John H. *Coleridge as Philosopher.* London, 1930. (Reprinted 1954).

Müller, Karl. *Friedrich Schlegels Konversion im Zusammenhang seiner weltanschaulichen Entwicklung.* Giessen, 1928.

Nemoianu, Virgil. *The Taming of Romanticism: European Literature in the Age of Biedermeier.* Cambridge, Mass., 1984.

Newe, Heinrich. "Die Philosophie Friedrich Schlegels in der Jahren 1804–1806." *Philosophisches Jahrbuch der Görresgesellschaft* 43, no. 3 (1930): 272–87.

Novalis. *Novalis.* Vol. 1: *Das dichterische Werk. Tagenbücher und Briefe.* Ed. Richard Samuel. Munich, 1978.

———. *Novalis.* Vol. 2: *Das philosophisch-theoretische Werk.* Ed. Hans-Joachim Mähl. Munich, 1978.

———. *Hymns to the Night.* Trans. Mabel Cotterell. London, 1948.

———. *Hymns to the Night.* Trans. Richard C. Higgins. 3d ed. New York, 1988.

———. *Hymns to the Night and Other Selected Writings.* Trans. Charles E. Passage. New York, 1960.

————. *The Novices of Sais*. Trans. Ralph Manheim. New York, 1949.

Novalis et al. *Novalis Schriften*. Ed. Paul Kluckhohn and Richard Samuel. 4 vols. Leipzig, 1929.

Ogden, John T. "The Structure of Imaginative Experience in Wordsworth's Prelude." *Wordsworth Circle* 6, no. 4 (Autumn 1975): 290–98.

Passage, Charles E. Introduction to *Hymns to the Night and Other Selected Writings*, by Novalis. Trans. Charles E. Passage. New York, 1960.

Pasternak, Boris. *Avtobiograficheskii ocherk: Proza*. Ann Arbor, Mich., 1961.

Peckham, Morse. "Constable and Wordsworth." In his *Collected Essays: The Triumph of Romanticism*. Columbia, S.C., 1970.

Piper, Herbert W. *The Active Universe: Pantheism and the Concept of Imagination in the English Romantic Poets*. London, 1962.

Pirie, Donald. "The Agony in the Garden: Polish Romanticism." In *Romanticism in National Context*, ed. Roy Porter and Mikulas Teich. New York, 1988.

Pottle, Frederick A. "The Eye and the Object in the Poetry of Wordsworth." In *Wordsworth Centenary Studies Presented at Cornell and Princeton Universities*, ed. Gilbert T. Dunklin. Princeton, N.J., 1951.

————. "Wordsworth in the Present Day." In *Proceedings of the American Philosophical Society* 115, no. 6 (December 21, 1972): 443–49.

Porter, Roy, and Mikulas Teich, eds. *Romanticism in National Context*. New York, 1988.

Poulet, Georges. *Les Métamorphoses du cercle*. Paris, 1961.

Pratt, Sarah. *Russian Metaphysical Romanticism: The Poetry of Tiutchev and Boratynskii*. Stanford, Calif., 1984.

Preitz, M., ed. *Friedrich Schlegel und Novalis: Biographie einer Romantikerfreundschaft in ihren Briefen*. Darmstadt, 1957.

Prichett, Steven. *Wordsworth and Coleridge: "The Lyrical Ballads."* London, 1975.

Ransom, John Crowe. "William Wordsworth: Notes Toward an Understanding of Poetry." In *Wordsworth Centenary Studies Presented at Cornell and Princeton Universities*, ed. Gilbert T. Dunklin. Princeton, 1951.

Raysor, Thomas M. "The Themes of Immortality and Natural Piety in Wordsworth's Immortality Ode." *Publications of the Modern Language Association of America* 69 (Sept.–Dec. 1954): 861–75.

Redeker, Martin. *Friedrich Schleiermacher: Leben und Werk (1768 bis 1834)*. Berlin, 1968.

Reed, Mark L. *Wordsworth: The Chronology of the Early Years, 1770–1799*. Cambridge, Mass., 1967.

————. *Wordsworth: The Chronology of the Middle Years, 1800–1815*. Cambridge, Mass., 1975.

Rehm, Walter. *Orpheus. Der Dichter und die Toten: Selbstdeutung und Totenkult bei Novalis–Hölderlin–Kleist*. Düsseldorf, 1950.

Riasanovsky, Nicholas V. "A. S. Khomiakov's Religious Thought." *St. Vladimir's Theological Quarterly* 23, no. 2 (1979): 87–100.

————. "The Emergence of Eurasianism." *California Slavic Studies* 4 (1967): 39–72.

————. *The Image of Peter the Great in Russian History and Thought*. New York, 1985.

————. "Khomiakov on *Sobornost'*." In *Continuity and Change in Russian and Soviet Thought*, ed. Ernest J. Simmons. Cambridge, Mass., 1955.

————. "On Lammenais, Chaadaev, and the Romantic Revolt in France and Russia." *American Historical Review* 82, no. 5 (Dec. 1977): 1165–86.

————. *Recent Scholarship on the Slavophiles*. The 30th Bernard Moses Memorial Lecture. Berkeley, Calif., 1985.

————. *Russia and the West in the Teaching of the Slavophiles: A Study of Romantic Ideology.* Cambridge, Mass., 1952.

————. *Russland und der Westen, Die Lehre der Slawophilen: Studie über eine romantische Ideologie.* Munich, 1954.

Richards, I. A. *Coleridge on Imagination.* New York, 1950.

Ritter, Heinz. *Der unbekannte Novalis: Friedrich von Hardenberg im Spiegel seiner Dichtung.* Göttingen, 1967.

Schanze, Helmut. *Romantik und Aufklärung: Untersuchungen zu Friederich Schlegel und Novalis.* 2d ed. Nuremberg, 1976.

Schenk, Hans G. *The Mind of the European Romantics: An Essay in Cultural History.* London, 1966.

Schlagdenhauffen, Alfred. *Frédéric Schlegel et son groupe: La Doctrine de l'Athenaeum (1798–1800).* Paris, 1934.

Schlegel, Friedrich. *Dialogue on Poetry and Literary Aphorisms.* Ed. E. Behler and R. Struc. University Park, Pa., 1968.

————. *Friedrich Schlegel. Schriften und Fragmente. Ein Gesamtbild seines Geistes.* Ed. Ernst Behler. Stuttgart, 1956.

————. *Friedrich Schelegel's "Lucinde" and the Fragments.* Trans. Peter Firchow. Minneapolis, 1971.

————. *Kritische Friedrich-Schlegel-Ausgabe.* ed. Ernst Behler. Munich, 1958–91, 35 vols.

————. *Literary Notebooks, 1797–1801.* Ed. Hans Eichner. London, 1957.

————. *Philosophische Vorlesungen [1800–1807] Erster Teil.* Ed. Jean-Jacques Austett. Kritische Friedrich-Schlegel-Ausgabe, vol. 12. Munich, 1964.

————. *Über die Sprache und Weisheit der Indier.* Ed. Ernst Behler and Ursula Struc-Oppenberg, Kritische Friedrich-Schlegel-Ausgabe, vol. 8 (Munich, 1975).

Schleiermacher, Friedrich. *Monologen.* [Berlin,] 1800.

————. *On Religion: Speeches to Its Cultured Despisers.* Trans. John Oman. New York, 1958.

————. *Über die Religion: Reden an die Gebildeten unter ihren Verächtern.* [Berlin,] 1979.

Schmitt, Carl. *Politische Romantik.* Munich, 1925.

Schulz, Gerhard. *Novalis in Selbstzeugnissen und Bilddokumenten.* Hamburg, 1969.

Setschkareff, Wsewolod. *Schellings Einfluss id der russichen Literatur der 20er und 30er Jahre des XIX Jahrhunderts.* Berlin, 1939.

Shaffer, E. S. *"Kubla Khan" and "The Fall of Jerusalem": The Mythological School in Biblical Criticism and Secular Literature, 1770–1880.* New York, 1975.

Silz, Walter. *Early German Romanticism. Its Founders and Heinrich von Kleist.* Cambridge, Mass., 1929.

Siskin, Clifford. *The Historicity of Romantic Discourse.* New York, 1988.

Sperry, Willard, L. *Wordsworth's Anti-Climax.* New York, 1966.

Stallknecht, Newton P. *Strange Seas of Thought: Studies in William Wordsworth's Philosophy of Man and Nature.* 2d ed. Bloomington, Ind., 1958.

Stepun, F. A. "Deutsche Romantik und Die Geschichtsphilosophie der Slawophilen." *Logos* (1927): 46–67.

————. "Nemetskii romantizm i russkoe slavianofilstvo." *Russkaia mysl* (March 1910): 65–91.

Stohschneider-Kohrs, Ingrid. *Die romantische Ironie in Theorie und Gestaltung.* Tübingen, 1960.

Strich, Fritz. *Deutsche Klassik und Romantik oder Vollendung und Unendlichkeit, ein Vergleich.* 3d ed. Munich, 1928.

Teich, Mikulas, and Roy Porter, eds. *Romanticism in National Context*. New York, 1988.

Tieck, Ludwig (and Wilhelm Heinrich Wackenroder). *Herzensergiessungen eines kunstliebenden Klösterbruders. And: Phantasien über die Kunst für Freunde der Kunst*. Ed. by A. Gillies. Oxford, 1948.

Tiutchev, F. I. *Polnoe sobranie sochinenii*. Ed. P. V. Bykov. St. Petersburg, 1913.

Trilling, Lionel. "The Immortality Ode," in his *Liberal Imagination*. Garden City, N.Y., 1953.

Triomphe, Robert. *Joseph de Maistre: Étude sur la vie et sur la doctrine d'un matérialiste mystique*. Geneva, 1968.

Tuveson, Ernest Lee. *The Avatars of Thrice Great Hermes*. Lewisburg, Pa., 1982.

———. *The Imagination as a Means of Grace: Locke and the Aesthetics of Romanticism*. Berkeley, 1960.

Viatte, Auguste. *Le Catholicisme chez les romantiques*. Paris, 1922.

Wackenroder, Wilhelm Heinrich (and Ludwig Tieck). *Herzensergiessungen eines kunstliebenden Klösterbruders* together with Wackenroder's contribution to the *Phantasien über die Kunst für Freunde der Kunst,* ed. A. Gillies. Oxford, 1948.

Walicki, Andrzej. *Philosophy and Romantic Nationalism: The Case of Poland*. Oxford, 1982.

———. *The Slavophile Controversy: History of a Conservative Utopia in Nineteenth Century Russian Thought*. Oxford, 1975.

Warren, Robert Penn. "A Poem of Pure Imagination: An Experiment in Reading," In *The Rime of the Ancient Mariner,* by Samuel Taylor Coleridge. New York, n.d.

Weissman, Stephen M., M.D. *His Brother's Keeper: A Psychobiography of Samuel Taylor Coleridge*. Madison, Conn., 1988.

Wellek, René. "The Concept of Romanticism in Literary History." In *Romanticism Reexamined: Concepts of Criticism*. Ed. Stephen G. Nichols, Jr. New Haven, Conn., 1962.

———. *Confrontations: Studies in the Intellectual and Literary Relations between Germany, England, and the United States During the Nineteenth Century*. Princeton, N.J., 1965.

Wiese, Benno von. *Friedrich Schlegel: Ein Beitrag zur Geschichte der romantischen Konversionen*. Berlin, 1927.

Wordsworth, Jonathan. *The Music of Humanity: A Critical Study of Wordsworth's "Ruined Cottage" Incorporating Texts from a Manuscript of 1799–1800*. London, 1969.

Wordsworth, William. *Poems*. Ed. John O. Hayden. Harmondsworth, England, 1977.

———. *The Poetical Works of William Wordsworth*. Ed. E. de Selincourt and Helen Darbishire. 5 vols. Oxford, 1940–49.

———. *The Poetical Works of Wordsworth*. Rev. ed., ed Paul D. Sheats. Boston, 1982.

———. *"The Prelude," 1799, 1805, 1850*. Ed. Jonathan Wordsworth, M. H. Abrams, and Stephen Gill. New York, 1979.

———. *The Prose Works of William Wordsworth*. 3 vols. Ed. W. J. B. Owen and James Worthington Smyser. Oxford, 1974.

Wordsworth, William, and Coleridge, Samuel Taylor. *Lyrical Ballads. The text of the 1798 edition with the additional 1800 poems and the Prefaces*. Ed. R. L. Brett and A. R. Jones. London, 1963.

Wordsworth, William, and Mary Wordsworth. *The Love Letters of William and Mary Wordsworth*. Ed. Beth Darlington, Ithaca, N.Y. 1981.

Index